WHAT ARE PEO[ ]
ABOUT THIS

C000084425

"The ability to sense and seize a destiny moment is a vital key to manifesting everything that God has assigned to your life. In JAVEN's new book *Do It NOW*, he provides an effective toolkit to show you how to do just that. I highly recommend it."

Touré Roberts
Author of Wholeness: Winning in Life from the Inside Out

"The most valuable thing you're given in life is time and the ultimate gift of time is your NOW! JAVEN has done a superb job in breaking down the importance and understanding of how to live in your NOW. *Do It NOW* will both empower you & inspire you to get up and make it happen!"

Paula White
Best Selling Author & TV Host

"Yesterday is gone and tomorrow is not promised, that's why your NOW is the most valuable time you have. I like that JAVEN is bringing us into remembrance of why our NOW moment is the most important one. In *Do It NOW,* you get a chance to be inspired, uplifted and directed on how to advance your purpose by living in the NOW."

Samuel Rodriguez
Best Selling Author & Speaker

"*Do It NOW* is amazing. I love the way JAVEN ignites the fire in us to get up, say goodbye to the past, be present in the moment and live the life we were designed to live. If you're ready to take life to a whole new level, you will LOVE this book!"

April Osteen Simons
Author & Speaker

"JAVEN represents a generation of introspective faith leaders who think deeply, process intently, and share freely. Without pretense and religious jargon JAVEN teaches us the rewards of a life fueled by faith and personal responsibility. You will enjoy his journey while reflecting on your own. This book will surely encourage you to live and move intently in your NOW!"

Terrell Fletcher
Author, Pastor, Former NFL'er

"Now is the time to make a change. Today is all we have. Yesterday is over and tomorrow is not here. There is really only today. In his powerful new book *Do It NOW,* JAVEN teaches us how we can make the most out of the moment."

Dr. Dave Martin
Best Selling Author & Speaker

DO IT

N🕐W

Why Wait for Better
When Your Best is Now?

JAVEN

Trilogy Christian Publishers A Wholly Owned Subsidiary of Trinity Broadcasting Network 2442 Michelle Drive Tustin, CA 92780

Rights Department, 2442 Michelle Drive, Tustin, CA 92780.

Trilogy Christian Publishing/ TBN and colophon are trademarks of Trinity Broadcasting Network.

For information about special discounts for bulk purchases, please contact Trilogy Christian Publishing.

Trilogy Disclaimer: The views and content expressed in this book are those of the author and may not necessarily reflect the views and doctrine of Trilogy Christian Publishing or the Trinity Broadcasting Network.

Manufactured in the United States of America

10 9 8 7 6 5 4 3 2 1

Library of Congress Cataloging-in-Publication Data is available.

B-ISBN: 978-1-68556-721-7

E-ISBN: 978-1-68556-722-4

SEL027000 SELF-HELP / Personal Growth / Success

BUS107000 BUSINESS & ECONOMICS / Personal Success

BUS019000 BUSINESS & ECONOMICS / Decision-Making & Problem Solving

CONTENTS

FOREWORD

Why wait for better when your best is NOW? It's a question we all should consider, and I cannot think of anyone more qualified to provide the answer than my good friend, JAVEN Campbell. As an accomplished producer, singer and public speaker, JAVEN has "been there, and done that." He's seen the highs, and he's experienced many of the lows.

Through it all he's discovered the middle ground that leads to success, and it's called the NOW! In *Do It NOW*, JAVEN takes us on a journey of learning what it means to live in the NOW—not considering the past or fretting about the future. He shares that living your best life is living within the NOW Season and the NOW Moment—knowing that you're exactly where you're supposed to be, and doing exactly what you're supposed to be doing with exactly the people you're supposed to be doing it with. JAVEN shows you that living the NOW way of life is all about how to act in the present in order to change the trajectory of your future.

He writes: "Knowing and embracing your Now is a subject that I think we all should try to connect to because it really is the midpoint of where our life connects."

If the past is over and the future has not taken place yet, then it's your NOW that becomes the center of your existence." This book is a must-read—not just for some, but for anyone who desires to make their best days count NOW!"

Henry Fernandez
Senior Pastor, Author & TV Host
The Faith Center, Sunrise, FL

INTRODUCTION

One of my guilty pleasures is watching the old black and white movies and TV shows. I like to see the movie stars of great films and TV shows from back in the day do their thing. Watching them accepting Oscars or Emmy Awards and doing appearances on talk shows, like Johnny Carson, I often wonder if they grasped the reality of the moment. If they knew that it was the best time of their life or had any clue that those incredible moments would one day be over and then become a memory and a part of history.

I also like to observe the great singers, musicians, and comedians. I study their body language, the way they laughed, or the words they chose. But I also use that same microscope in my own present life and ask myself, "Am I realizing my magical moments and the incredible life experiences I'm having? Am I making the best of my now season?"

The days with greats like Sinatra, Don Rickles, and Ella Fitzgerald are long gone, never to return. Their moments to take in their now will never happen again—hopefully they did just that while they had the chance. I can't help but wonder how many of us make the same mistake of going day after day, moment after moment, experience after experience, forgetting to embrace our now. We forget to acknowledge how blessed we are to have had that particular moment or experience. I once heard someone say, "When you are at the end of your life, and are about to take your final breath, your money, the size of your house, or how many cars you have won't matter. But what you will think about are the people you have loved and the purpose you would have fulfilled, or the lack thereof."

Knowing and embracing your Now is a subject that I think we all should try to connect to because it really is the midpoint of where our life connects. If the past is over and the future has not taken place yet, then it's your Now that becomes the center of your existence.

The other day I journeyed down a street that had a cemetery next to it. The street was very calm and peaceful, but to my surprise, there were people jogging in the cemetery as if it were a normal park. In their defense, the quietude and cleanliness of that small graveyard, that seemingly had about 100 grave sites, was so alluring and welcoming that anyone would want to walk, drive, or jog through it. It intrigued me so much that I myself decided to drive through it. As I slowly drove through, I began doing the first thing anyone would do: I started to read the headstones. I wondered how old the people were when they died. As I captured dates on various monuments, I started to calculate ages based on the year of birth and the year of death. Some went back as far as 1914 and 1912. Some were as recent as 2014 and 2015. I particularly noticed one stone of an athlete—a football player who was born in 1988 and died in 2001. When I did the math on his age, I realized how little time he had had on this earth.

That experience made me leave that place knowing that whatever I needed to get done for that particular day had to be completed, that not only was I not to be afraid to do it, but I was meant to do it. I was already connected to it and it was connected to me. My first priority was to pay attention to what was immediately before me in that now moment and what it meant to accomplish it. I then suddenly had the urge to do a responsibility check, to make sure that I had not slipped into my past thoughts, my past failures, or past disappointments. I needed to do an inventory of any thoughts of anxiety from being impatient while waiting on what is to come. I also began to challenge myself to fully be engrafted into my responsibilities, no matter how boring they may be or however they may be lacking—I am to embrace it, love it, entertain it, and allow it to entertain me. It was my moment of getting to a place of fulfillment, knowing that I am doing exactly what I'm supposed to be doing, because I'm exactly where I'm supposed to be. I think that's what the now is all about: knowing that you're exactly where you're supposed to be, doing exactly what you're supposed to be doing with exactly the people you're supposed to be doing it with. I believe that if we embrace that, it begins the opportunity for a better, greater, more rounded, diversified you, and that, my friend, is living in the Now.

As a producer, singer, and speaker for almost twenty years, I have enjoyed bringing purposeful entertainment to audiences around the world. I've been blessed to have performed on Broadway and appeared in several films as an actor. I continue to produce and host TV shows and have received accolades as a recording artist. It has been, and continues to be, a blessed life.

Along the way, I have met and talked with thousands of people. Because of my own journey to create a blessed life for myself, many people come to me hoping to learn how they can improve their own lives. It is humbling. I am not necessarily a wise man; I'm just a person who is always interested in the reason we are who we are and why we are where we are. You see, I believe the Now way of life is all about how to act in the present in order to change the trajectory of your future.

These days, much of my time is spent sharing the message of Now with people globally through insightful and meaningful conversations that uplift people and teach a different—and I believe better—way to live. I do this with music, speaking, producing, and a host of other activities. All are designed to create exchanges that will answer questions like:

- Why does my life seem meaningless?
- Why can't I stop letting the past get in my way?
- Why am I living less than I ought to?
- Why don't I have time to pursue my passion?

I have come to believe that the answers to these "why" questions are rooted in understanding the message of Now. I would like to show you exactly how to answer life's challenges and find more. Now is a way of looking at things that will permeate every aspect of your life. It is both simple and complex. It will fill you with laughter and tears. It is a philosophy that I believe with all my heart and soul is profound and life-giving.

"Wait a minute," you may say. "I know all about living in the moment. I'm actually an expert at it. I have no plans for the future. It's all about getting through the day."

That's not what I am talking about. Now is not about time. Now is about purpose. Think of it as living in the most extraordinary season of your life in a conscious, deliberate manner. Right Now. Your Now Season. Can you imagine the results if you truly gave that purpose-filled season your absolute all?

What if, as moms and dads, you actually focused on your children during your child-raising season? That would mean looking away from your cell phone and trying to play with and teach them. What if, as an entrepreneur, you devoted your energy in all positive and possible ways to achieve success in your start-up season? That would mean not getting sidetracked by hobbies until your business was up and running. Or what if, as a person suffering a loss, you put no time limits on your pain and did not let others pressure you to "get over it" during your grieving season? You could then allow yourself to move on with an appreciation of life because you have healed.

One reason I believe I have something important to share with you is because of my experiences with so many people from all walks of life. People who have suffered tragedies. Youth who are adrift. Widows and widowers whose light has gone out. Husbands and wives who no longer feel connected. Parents who don't understand how their kids have strayed onto a bad path. Children who feel unloved and unappreciated. Men and women afraid of the future.

The other reason I feel qualified to write this book is because of my own experiences, which I will be sharing candidly throughout this book. I want you to see the mistakes I have made and the roads that brought me sorrow, even when it looked to the world as though I were at the top of my game. I want to share what I have learned because so many of the lessons may apply to what you are facing today. Some of my stories, like yours, may make you laugh. Others, like yours, may make you cry. But my focus is purposeful: to share with you what I have learned that has shaped me into the man I am today. Let me start by telling you a bit more about me.

I have a passion for music. It grounds me in the moment like nothing else can. In fact, I think musicians are able to understand living in the Now better than many other people. Because when you are on a stage performing, you can't think about what you did the day before or what you are going to do after the performance. You have to be in the moment because if you are not, your performance will suffer.

At one point, music was all encompassing for me. It was my Now Season of music. It led me into acting, which also became my Now Season. Performing was my livelihood, and I dedicated myself to it wholeheartedly. It even enabled me to be an engaged and successful single parent. I will tell you much more about that later in this book.

Today my Now Season has changed once again. I am totally absorbed in using all my talents and experiences as a leader, speaker, producer, and TV host to help others—no matter where they have come from or where they are at present—to find hope, purpose, and direction. I want them to know what I know. I believe that we are all students of knowledge and should be constant learners. But while our perceptions change as we live and experience life, we still need core principles that guide our life so that we can be teachers and leaders for our families, children, friends, and communities.

Equally important, we need to act on those principles. While understanding is important, it is even more important to learn how to turn that understanding into meaningful actions. That's why this book is designed to spur you into action and then continue to support and inspire you. To that end, I will show you:

- How to live a purposeful Now
- How to fully embrace the present
- How to learn from the past without getting stuck there
- How to stay open to possibilities
- How to overcome obstacles in your life
- How to gain an attitude of gratitude
- How to tap into your faith

My sincere hope is that by sharing what I have learned, you in turn will learn the life lesson that has changed me and thousands of people: *how to act purposely in the present.*

I suggest that you read this book from beginning to end. At the end of each chapter, I have included practice exercises to help guide you; summaries of key points; and Wisdom Keys, inspirational summary statements about The Now Way of Life to expand your thinking and generate insight and wisdom.

You may want to write down your own thoughts as you read. Putting pen to paper or creating an online journal is a powerful way to reflect on and capture your feelings. It will also help you move forward with action, which is an essential part of any transformational journey.

Please approach Do it *NOW: Why wait for better when your best is NOW* with openness and joy. As you walk through this journey, know that I am right by your side.

CHAPTER ONE

THE NOW WAY OF LIFE

What is real success? I can tell you exactly what it is not. Success is not money, fortune, or fame. It is not a fancy car or vacation home. Someone once said, "Money doesn't make you better; it just makes you more of what you already were." Just look at statistics in the NBA, NFL, MLB, and more. You will find the numbers staggering of all the players who squandered millions. Many are left in debt and bankruptcy; others live on government assistance.

The reality is that many of us don't know how to handle our successes. Instead of helping us attain stability and achievement, our successes magnify the unfinished business within ourselves that we have yet to work on. If there are flaws and bad habits in our lives, success multiplies them.

Think about defining success as fulfilling your purpose in what I call your Now Season. We all have multiple Now Seasons in our lives. For example, there is the season of raising your family. There is the season of building a successful career. There is the season of being a leader in your community.

Yes, these seasons overlap. But unless we focus on the primary purpose of a particular season and complete the assignments and tasks required for that time, we will not be happy. If you are trying to build a successful career when your assignment is to focus on your newborn baby and wife, you will not be successful. Why? Because you are not acting purposefully in the present.

I don't know anyone who wants **to** be unsuccessful. Most people want to have a successful life, and they certainly don't want it to get worse. If anything, they want it to get better. In my experience, the reason why somebody can live a lifetime without things getting better is because they never recognized their Now Season and lived on purpose in it. They did not know how to.

I specifically use the language "live *on* purpose" not "live *with* purpose." Everything I'm doing, I'm doing on purpose. For example, I'm purposefully getting to bed early because this is a time for physical rest, as I know I'm taking on too much mentally.

Additionally, we sometimes assume that anything that seems admirable or positive is good for us. That's just not true. I know many actors who never had another hit movie after winning an Oscar. I know too many one-hit-wonder singers. I know of people who won the lottery and became overnight millionaires, only to be transformed into the worst version of themselves and end up in poverty.

We get caught up in our spotlight moments and don't feel the need to keep pushing forward to keep achieving and maintaining character, strength, and humility. When you consider success, take a look back and ask yourself, "How did that achievement hurt me?" or "How did it work to my disadvantage?"

Some folks call this attitude "keeping your feet on the ground." But I like the words of Winston Churchill: "Success is not final. Failure is not fatal. It is the courage to continue that counts."

Living on Purpose

Living in the Now means you are living on purpose. You are living in the direct consciousness of saying, "How do I want to make this Now Season work for me? What do I want to receive from it? How can I grow in it?"

If you don't answer these questions, then your actions will not be purposeful. It's the throw-anything-at-the-wall-and-see-what-sticks approach. You are relying on luck or chance. You live based on what the world, economy, political system, or people around you say about your situation.

> WISDOM KEY
>
> LIVE ON PURPOSE, NOT JUST WITH PURPOSE

Wouldn't it be nice if you could make decisions about your life independently and intentionally, if you could define success as whatever it may be for you? I'm not talking about having a fancy car or a big house; I'm saying that whatever you have, you find the purpose in it.

When you live in the Now, you also have the opportunity to learn from your current situation. Every circumstance you face—every battle and struggle—is an opportunity to learn, grow, and mature, and a chance for us to position ourselves for greater success.

This doesn't mean you don't have tough times. There are no certainties in this life other than the choices we make to deal with whatever it is we are facing. Purpose is not developed because you go through something. Purpose is already there. The essential thing is how you position yourself throughout the situation.

One important thing to remember is this: You do not need to go through a situation alone. I liken it to fitness. You can have the right mind and heart to work out, build muscle, and get lean. But if you get on that bench under too many of those weights, without a coach or spotter, you can hurt yourself.

Now put that in the framework of a season in your life. When you can't handle what life is throwing at you, whether it be your children, finances, or emotions, then it may be time to recognize that you need counseling or other support to help you. You might need to explore your spiritual journey and make time for prayer. You might want to join a local women's group.

In my work, I often talk with mothers who are at home with young children. They express feelings of isolation and lack of self-worth, and even talk about feeling distanced from their babies. This is a horrible situation for both the mothers and their children; it can be avoided if they find spotters among other young mothers. It comes from this understanding: "I'm not a working mother. I'm not a traveling single person anymore. I'm not just a wife anymore. I'm a mother. I'm responsible for a child. This might be too much for me. Let me connect with others who are dealing with that."

That's finding a spotter. That's having somebody help you lift the weights as you are getting fit. Living in the Now is saying, "I will need help at certain seasons in my life."

Changing with Each Now Season

Living in the Now is never one thing. Different seasons require different positions. Living in the Now means, "I am everything, and at the same time I am nothing." Living in the Now says, "I need help, and at the same time I might be able to be of help to someone."

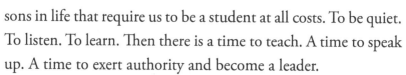

WISDOM KEY

CHANGE COMES TO THOSE WHO ARE STILL LIVING, SO EXPECT IT

It is about what is needed for that time, what is needed for that season. There are seasons in life that require us to be a student at all costs. To be quiet. To listen. To learn. Then there is a time to teach. A time to speak up. A time to exert authority and become a leader.

The Now Way of Living focuses on approach, flexibility, and intention. The approach is about purpose. Your approach may change based on a situation. There was a time I had to be very assertive in making business decisions. As an independent artist,

I was the manager, booking agent, writer, publisher, producer, publicist, and finance person. I didn't have the luxury of people working for me, so I had to be assertive in getting things done.

As my career developed, I began to have managers, producers, and labels. At first, it was a bit hard for me to let go of some of those responsibilities. But the more I learned how to let go, get out of the way, and let other people do their jobs, not only did my load get lighter, but my music and artistry flourished.

I repositioned myself from being wrapped up in the business to being an artist. This did not mean that I became passive, but rather I focused on the purpose of being completely myself as an artist, delivering great music, and being there for the fans.

So many things in our lives require us to have different approaches to different seasons. You won't know that, however, if you're not living in the Now. You'll breeze through a season only to find that you missed incredible moments that could have positioned you in a healthier way to face your future. If you live in the Now, these moments will provide strength, wisdom, and knowledge that will secure your future.

However, if you don't have this awareness, you become a person who has been exposed to a lot of things but never really experiences them. Think of it this way. I see you, but I didn't see you. I was there, but I didn't really know what was going on. I was a part of that, but I really was not experiencing whatever was happening.

This is what I firmly believe: It's important for us to live with this approach so that we can have a full life. Someone can claim,

"I've been married for fifty years." But did he have a successful marriage for fifty years, or was it just something on paper? Another person can say, "I've been living for thirty years." Has she been really living or just existing, just breathing? Here's what living in the Now does for us: it helps us become participants rather than bystanders in life.

Gaining Wisdom by Living in the Now

Wisdom is applied knowledge for a guaranteed result. You would think that wisdom would kick in automatically like an alarm clock in your head, but instead, it must be turned on almost like a key in a car ignition. Common sense will tell you that if you do things a certain way, you are going to get a certain result. Unfortunately, common sense is not that common when we are faced with tragedies and disappointments in life.

Wisdom requires memory, knowledge, and a healthy balance to one of the most important questions in everyday life: "What do I want this outcome to be?" Wisdom comes into play when the information that is received is understood and then acted upon without going through the same bad experience again and again. It was Albert Einstein who said, "We can't solve problems by using the same kind of thinking we used when we created them."

Let's look at this scenario. You relocated to a new community where you had a brief conversation with your 84-year-old next-door neighbor. He told you not to walk alone on a particular road after 7 p.m. on the weekdays. That's knowledge.

You didn't listen, so you went for a stroll in the cool night air under the starry, clear sky. As you came upon the road you were warned not to tread, you noticed two suspicious men lurking, so you turned away before being threatened. That's understanding.

The next week when it's time to take your walk, you make sure you take a totally different route. That's wisdom. Of course, had you listened to your 84-year-old neighbor in the first place, you would have never dealt with the situation because he might have been a victim and was sharing his knowledge with you.

WISDOM KEY

LIFE GETS HARDER WHEN YOU FIGHT IT AND EASIER WHEN YOU EMBRACE IT

Many of us think we have to touch the freshly painted wall to see if it's really wet even after being told not to. We call that learning the hard way. Is it wise to have experiences to gain wisdom, or is it wise to learn from those who have already been through them? Why would you want to go through something when you can learn from a person who already experienced it?

Whether you learn from what you are told or from your own experiences, wisdom will start navigating you from hurts, pains, bad decisions, and disappointments.

Wisdom gives you an eagle's eye, allowing you to see things coming from a mile away. It reminds you that you've taken that road before, and you don't have to take it again. If you don't know how wisdom can really work for your good, you will be in trouble. This is why many of us keep having repeats of yesterdays. We keep thinking that our misfortunes were merely mistakes, and so we don't capture the lessons of what they were really teaching us.

Opportunities Surround Us

Living in the Now means pushing past your past and grabbing the next opportunity that's standing right in front of you. Someone is always ready to take over where someone else has left off. Opportune moments and conditions surround us daily, and they are found in the most unlikely places. They come through the most unassuming people and can be seen in the most unimaginable situations.

They are not allocated for one person, and they don't have unilateral assignments. Opportunity can come in simplicity, in the form of hard work, and will even stand right before your eyes, looking like something else you never could imagine. If you know what to look for, you'll never miss your opportunity to do something great.

The best opportunities hide in the worst situations. There are seeds of growth in every problem you face. So the next time you are faced with a problem, remember that it is just an opportunity to gain more seeds to sow and grow from.

There's a story about a young man who wished to marry a farmer's beautiful daughter, so he went to ask for permission. The farmer thought he had to prove himself worthy. "Son," he said, "Go stand out in that field, and I'm going to release three bulls, one at a time. If you can catch the tail of any of the three bulls, then you can marry my daughter."

The young man stood in the pasture and waited for the first bull. The barn door opened and out came the biggest, meanest-looking bull he had ever seen. He decided that one of the next bulls had to be a better choice than the first one, so he ran over to the side and let the bull pass through the pasture and out the back gate.

The barn door opened a second time, and to his astonishment, an even bigger and fiercer bull came through. It stood pawing the ground, grunting, slinging slobber as it eyed him. "Whatever the next bull is like, it has to be a better choice than this one," the young man thought. So, he ran to the fence, and the bull went out through the back gate.

The door then opened for the third time. A smile lit up his face: it was the weakest, scrawniest little bull he had ever seen. "This is it. This is my bull!" he thought. As the bull came running by, he threw out his hands and grabbed toward the bull's rear, but to his surprise, there was no tail.

Waiting for what seemed to be the right opportunity cost him the dream of marrying his beautiful bride. So many people miss their dream because they waited too long on the "right" opportunity. We all can move forward by taking the opportunities before us, but many of us are waiting on the small bull to run by so we can then grab the tail. The truth is, that small bull is not the right opportunity; it's the other two that you already let run past you because you thought they were too big or risky for you.

As you begin to climb the ladder of success, it will increase your positive feelings about the course you are on. Don't hold on to what should've been but rather look for the value in your today, things that will clear the cloud to your future. It's up to you to take control of today and become a pioneer of your tomorrow.

To become the pioneers of our tomorrows, we have to reflect on our own story and history. In the next chapter, I will share my path to The Now Way of Life as well as some of the lessons I have learned along the way.

In Summary

Your Now Season refers to the multiple times in your life when your attention needs to be focused on what is going on right now. Your energy and commitment need to be directed at achieving a primary purpose like raising a child, starting a business, or taking care of an aging parent.

Living on purpose means the everyday actions you take to be aware and move purposefully through your Now Season. For example, getting enough sleep if you are under stress, seeking help from others, or spending more time with your family. As you move through your Now Season, you gain wisdom from knowledge and insights. This allows you to seize opportunities and move on to greater things in your life.

Practice

Try answering the following questions to give you insights into The Now Way of Life:

1. *What is your current Now Season?*

_____

_____

_____

_____

_____

_____

_____

_____

_____

_____

_____

_____

_____

_____

2. *What do you see as the purpose of your Now Season?*

3. *What are examples of how you are living on purpose?*

_____

_____

_____

_____

_____

_____

_____

_____

_____

_____

_____

_____

_____

CHAPTER TWO

MY PATH TO NOW

Everyone will come to a point in their life where they are in their own timeline. For me, realizing the importance of living in the Now evolved over a period of years. A combination of ups and downs and trials and errors culminated in my adopting The Now Way of Life and teaching others what I have learned.

For a long time—and still today—I have been a student of life. As I matured and became wiser, I was finally able to understand how I could find the answers to the challenges of life and share them in powerful ways with others.

I grew up in a very large, conservative family. My dad was a minister. Vacations consisted of driving three hours north to Disney World or going other places in Florida. I knew at a young age that I wanted to build a noteworthy career and travel the globe, but I always wanted to come back home to family.

I barely graduated from high school. The public school system did not work for me, and I did not do well with testing. Many kids today experience the same problems. But I knew that there was more, and I knew that I wanted a higher education. I just didn't know how to get there. I certainly didn't have the pedigree on paper. If you looked at my scores, grades, and patterns in school, you would say I was not college material. But in my senior year, I was absolutely ready to graduate and excited to begin my bright future.

When Your Life Takes a Dramatic Turn

Then I found out I was going to be a father. My vision of traveling, venturing out, and doing extraordinary things came to a halt. I lost hope of becoming a student and doing all the irresponsible things that 17-year-olds get a chance to do. I thought all that went out the window when I knew I was going to be responsible for a child.

I was devastated. I fell into a dark and depressed place while feeling the weight of disappointment and embarrassment that I caused my family. Then my mom sat me down at the kitchen table and said, "You know, you're not the first teenager to have a child, and you will not be the last. Everything's going to be all right. Your plan to go to college needs to stay the same, and you are going to go. We're going to help do whatever we can with this child, and we're going to get through this. Nothing changes. Keep going forward."

In her wisdom, she was telling her 17-year-old son to pursue his dreams, go to college, make success happen, and travel the world. I was still responsible for bringing a child into the world and would face unforeseen consequences for the next eighteen years, but she clearly saw that the path to take was to stay in my Now and move forward.

As a wiser adult reflecting on that moment, her words, "*Nothing changes; keep going forward*," became an integral part of my path to Now. Today I understand that while the decision point is at a crossroad, all roads still actually go in the same direction. My direction was to raise my son well. I could go right or I could go left. Both of them were going to take me to the same destination, but if I went right, it would give me one experience, and if I went left, it would give me another.

WISDOM KEY

YOU HAVE BEEN DESIGNED TO MOVE FORWARD

I've seen this in my life over and over again with many crucial Now Moments. Was I going to sink or swim? Was I going to pout and drag through it or hold my head up and figure it out? These crossroad situations happen to many of us. The difference is how we handle them. Do we see purpose in our Now Moment and press forward no matter what? Do we acknowledge the challenge while not letting it determine whether or not we go on?

These days, I think that sometimes it's just crazy faith or ridiculous hope that makes you move forward during tough times. In some ways, it's about ignoring your current reality. Unless you have a miracle, there is a good chance you're going to fail, and you're going to fail hard. So I absolutely believe in miracles.

I realized back then that if I didn't go to college, my life was going to be stuck in a rut for a long time. I knew I would look back with regret. So I applied to a school that I didn't think would accept me. But I did get in. That was a miracle.

I bought a one-way ticket to Tennessee with no real promise of having my tuition covered. The only thing that I had was the down payment for my dorm room. A month later, the door opened for me to get Pell grants, scholarships, and student loans. That was a miracle.

It took a huge leap of faith to buy that one-way ticket. Even as I write about this now, I'm thinking that it was a bit insane to do that. But I had so much fire, boldness, and faith. I remember thinking that if I had to come home because it didn't work out, at least people wouldn't say I didn't try.

My son was born during my first semester in college. I'd be lying if I told you it has been easy to raise him. Going to college was the first of many challenges. Nothing changed in my situation. I was still a dad. The only thing that changed was the way that I viewed that Now Moment.

You know, life is like a river. It keeps going, and you have to keep going with it. You don't have to go strong. You don't have to go perfect. You don't even have to know where you're going. All that matters is that you've made up your mind that you're going to continue on with the agenda at hand. You are going to move on down that river.

Because I am a living and breathing vessel, I have what it takes to stream down the river. I have what it takes to be at peace. I have what it takes to create and re-create. What I create may not be as big or rich as the last thing, but it's going to be something fresh and new. This belief creates an incredible pattern that is so important to your Now.

The Beginning of My Music Season

A few months after I got to college, I joined a professional music group where we went out on weekends to perform across the country. We always made it back by Monday for classes. This was the beginning of my professional music career. It literally changed the direction of my future, a future I thought would be in communications or journalism.

We didn't get paid much money, but for the first time, I was paid for something I did for fun—singing. If you grow up in a big family like mine, particularly where your parents are ministers, singing is commonplace. It's kind of a given that you will either sing or play an instrument. Up until this time, I did not see music as a profession; I saw it more as a hobby. So joining this professional band and being one of these frontline singers was big to me.

I wasn't a songwriter then; I didn't even choose the songs we were performing. But it was intensely challenging. I had to learn new music at the drop of a dime. I had to learn how to harmonize and not sing over others. I had to learn how to woo a crowd—how to get everybody involved in a song. I then began to understand and appreciate the stage and the ability to move a crowd through music.

That was just the music part. I also had to learn interpersonal skills: how to get along with band members, some of whom I didn't like, or who did not like me. Additionally, life on the road is not as glamorous as it seems. The glamorous part is the stage, but there's a grueling aspect behind the scene. Loading and unloading a tour bus of sound, staging, and production equipment. Brushing your teeth in truck stops and sometimes going without a shower. Getting dressed on the bus and sleeping in a bunk for hours while crossing the country. Singing, getting back on the bus, and then doing it all over again.

Having gone to college as a father with no financial backing, I certainly thought I was tough. But life got tougher when I began to pursue a professional music career.

Learning About Quitting

Our director was a hard taskmaster who would call you out on stage if you were singing flat or off key. He did not mince words. That rattled me, but also allowed me to either get in there and fight or quit and go home.

I'd love to tell you that I stuck with the band, but I didn't. I quit four or five times when I got upset. Each time, I would come back and finish what I had started because there was more for me to learn, particularly from the director, whom I now love. If he called today, I'd be on a plane to go see him.

So, quitting clearly wasn't about the band director. It was about what was taking place in me. It was about toughening a guy who thought he was tough. I was a father and had lost my own dad while in college. But I learned I wasn't as tough as I thought I was.

Looking back, I think there's something about having the option to leave the group that made the challenge greater and harder. I've learned that if you are forced into a situation and have no other choice, the options become simple. If it's a life and death situation, you go into survival mode. But in less dire situations when there are more options, responses can be more complex.

It's an extraordinary opportunity to endure while in these types of moments of having to choose to move forward or to quit. Do I choose to stay in a marriage or get out? Do I choose to excel at work or just get by? Do I choose to go to school or stay in a dead-end job? Do I choose to have a child or wait until I am financially stable? The list goes on and on.

You cannot become great until you're confronted with great trials, problems, or circumstances. And often, greatness is developed when we choose to stay instead of leaving when things get tough. That's when greatness is inspired and uplifted. Who wants goodness when you can have greatness? The enemy of great is good. Something might be good for you, but it may not be great for you. Choose greatness over goodness every day, and life will be extraordinarily great for you.

WISDOM KEY

YOU HAVE TO <u>INVEST</u> IN YOUR FUTURE. IF YOU WON'T, DON'T EXPECT THAT OTHERS WILL

When I made the decision to go back and finish with the band, it was a very tough choice, but I went anyway. After graduating from college, we did one final tour together, and it was incredible—playing in big arenas in China, Indonesia, all across the U.S.A, and Canada before thousands of people. Then I moved on with my career. This experience, however, set me up for greatness, and for the backbone I would need to endure in the very tough world I was about to enter.

My Next Now Season of Music

The next major test of my toughness came as a young adult in my early thirties when I left my job of ten years in Florida and went to pursue my dreams. I had not written any hit albums, but I worked hard on getting a record deal. I realized that if I did not do what I knew to do in that moment, then nothing was ever going to change for me. That is really what is so important about the Now Season. It's not so much about moving forward as it is about moving on. It's about taking that leap of faith. I had no real opportunities other than a big vision of what I could be.

> WISDOM KEY
>
> WEALTH IS NOT HOW MUCH MONEY YOU HAVE, BUT HOW MANY OPTIONS YOU HAVE

I packed everything that I owned and crossed the country to California to start a new life, leaving behind a three-bedroom home in a gated community with a Land Rover and BMW.

Judging only by material possessions, some people may see this as a pretty good life. Never the less I took another big leap of faith and moved on to start a new journey and a new life.

After moving to California, I lived in a Holiday Inn for three weeks, on Ventura Boulevard in Studio City, until I was able to move in to a two-bedroom apartment. I replaced my two cars with a less expensive one—a definite step down from my previous lifestyle. I crammed whatever furniture I could into that small apartment, not really knowing anybody or having any real connections. Looking back, it was a humbling moment for me, but you couldn't have told me that I had downgraded my life.

I won't say it was easy to make such a drastic and challenging move. But I didn't feel lonely. I didn't feel afraid. I didn't feel anything but excitement. I guess if something is personally exciting to you, it's not hard, it's just challenging. And when it's exciting, who doesn't like a challenge? That's one more thing that Now is all about—finding the excitement in the challenge.

You know, perception is not reality, but perception does create reality. My reality was that I was in a bubble—an atmosphere of excitement. If your atmosphere is an exciting place, it doesn't mean you will not have problems. It just means that you will view them as challenges you can overcome because of the excitement and passion you feel. I didn't know what would come, but I knew I was where I was supposed to be. I embraced my Now Season wholeheartedly, and it became the beginning of many beginnings.

In our Now, we have the ability to make powerful choices that can alter our destiny and future. We can either abort things by what we say or do, or give birth to great things by the choices we make. Great is the result of great effort or seeds of greatness sown.

It's naïve to think that you can get great results from little to no effort; to think you can do nothing and expect everything is just unrealistic. I'm not saying everybody has to pack up their house and move across the country, blindly taking steps of faith. But there is some element of risk that has to take place within your Now Season in order for you to start that journey of greatness. You have a right to your future. You have the liberty to your future. So, not only are you free to take it, you're obligated to take it. It is yours. It's only for you.

I made this move in my Now Season when I had already established a successful life in my thirties, with responsibilities— not as an 18-year-old kid with no children, house, or lifestyle. I do believe, however, that at any point in your life, you need to make a move if you know there's more.

I made the same choice when I started auditioning for movies. I started acting classes, took on an acting coach, and did hours upon hours of rehearsals. It was what I wanted to do. I'm not going to tell you that I got the part each time, but being turned down for a part only made me want to go back and work harder. My attitude was clear: If I don't do it now, I may never get another opportunity. I don't want to miss my moment.

You know, there isn't a textbook or equation for success in the entertainment industry. It's all based on creativity and connections. Sometimes it's just about hoping, wishing, and miracles. You can write a song and love it, but that doesn't mean everybody is going to like it. You can do your best performing, but it doesn't mean the audience is going to get it, like it, or even want to watch it.

We see this happen all the time in movies. There are so many that fail even though producers and studios have spent millions of dollars on them. They think audiences are going to connect, only to find out they don't. Honestly, it's about as close to gambling as anything.

> ### WISDOM KEY
>
> ## YOU HAVE TO FIRST LOVE THE <u>IDEA</u> OF WINNING IN ORDER TO <u>WIN</u>

After being in the entertainment industry for so many years, I can tell you it is a very tough life. It looks glamorous on the outside and results can be exhilarating, but the grind is extremely difficult. You need either an innate or learned ability to say that no matter what, you're going to get the job done. You have to make up in your mind that, "if this is the job where I'm at, the place that I'm supposed to be, the connection that I have to make, and the resources that I'm connected to, then no matter what, I'm going to get the job done."

Unfortunately, many people think that if it's not "winning," then it's not important. In the Now, there is no such thing as winning or losing. It's only purpose. Good and bad actually don't exist when you talk about purpose and have a greater meaning and reason for life. If you lose a relationship, it doesn't feel good, but it teaches you how to guide your heart in certain ways. It shows you how to be careful of the pitfalls and certainly gives you thicker skin.

It's so important that we are willing to take advantage of those moments because they open big doors that we will miss if we don't. So here is the question I have for you: are you missing your Now Moment? It doesn't have to be right. It doesn't have to be perfect. But you have to be fully in it, or you will potentially miss great opportunities. That's what I did. I took knowledge, grit, faith, and the Now philosophy and just went for it.

What Now

These days, I often work behind the scenes helping to produce shows and singers. In this capacity, I'm not what we call "the talent" or "the main artist." Rather, I connect the dots and put those pieces together for whatever we're doing. It still requires the decision to say, "I really have to stay with this no matter what."

My life today is productive with both fast and slow moments. Let me give you a taste of the fast-moving part. My company, jROCK Media, works with celebrity artists and musicians to put together award shows, movies, television productions, and other projects. A lot of this includes my own personal projects like live tv shows which I help to produce and co-host.

I also have a vibrant music career with eight national album releases. You can find me in the studio, sometimes until 3 a.m., writing and recording new music. And the promotion is intense with photo shoots, artwork, radio interviews, and making appearances.

Television is one way I get out the Now message. I produce and host a show called *Now Living* in the United Kingdom, flying to London twice a year to create episodes for the series. I also do an American version of the show where I feature celebrity guests talking about their Now Seasons.

I am on the road constantly, pitching new ideas, promoting, singing, speaking, and producing. Recently, I visited radio stations in eight cities in six states in just four days. It's a grueling schedule but very rewarding.

My slow days consist of being home and working with our local Now Church ministry on strategic planning and programs that involve everything from financial seminars to our annual Summer Slam Sport Camp for 200 underprivileged foster care youth. I really love this annual event because it reminds me how much my life is not about me but about our future. We pair the youth with mentors that include former NFL players, NBA players, coaches, and nurses to talk and teach them about health and wellness, and improve their leadership skills.

I continue teaching and studying on a regular basis. I do my best to bring information and revelation that I think will inspire and cause people to be strengthened in their faith and become better stewards of the blessings in their lives.

My family is massive, so there are continuous activities around birthdays, marriages, and graduations as well as supporting people through difficult times. At the heart is my precious mom. I am so intensely aware of this Now Season of her life where both her mind and body are fragile. I sit with her and let her know I love her. And, of course, there is always my son, now grown and on his own adventures. Thank you, FaceTime.

So you can see, my current Now Season is filled with purpose and action. Because I am fully living in the Now, I experience each moment with a richness that makes even the hard times beautiful. In the next chapter, I am going to share with you my thoughts about how you can wake up in the Now so that you too can have a wondrous life.

In Summary

My path to success has not been straightforward. There have been many twists and turns and many trials and tribulations. The one thing I want you to take away is that no matter what the situation, when you live in your Now Season and give it 1,000 percent, you will be able to capitalize on successful possibilities for your future.

Practice

Create three columns. In the first column, write down a major life event. For example, mine was moving from Florida to California. In the second column, write down the obstacles that you faced during that life event. For example, mine was losing a source of income. In the third column, write down the positive things you gained from that life event. For example, mine was jumpstarting my career as a musician, actor, and producer.

CHAPTER THREE

WAKING UP TO NOW

The reaction I usually get while lecturing and teaching on the Now is usually one of surprise and anticipation. Some people have just never thought about life in the Now. They tend to think in the past or future; very few think in the present. Even if they do, they don't see how it relates to the past or affects the future. So it really awakens something in people and becomes an "aha" moment for them when I begin to talk from this platform.

What I have learned is that people are hurting. They are disappointed, disconnected, and disenfranchised. They see other people's success, progression, and purpose but not their own. When I begin to talk about these topics, I see a light in their eyes. I see hope and a desire to hear and do more.

These are the statements that give me great joy and fulfillment:

"That really, really helped and encouraged me to do some things that I've just kind of been putting on the back burner."

"From now on, I won't allow fear to hold me back. I will move forward."

"I didn't know what to do, so I was procrastinating. Now I won't."

When they have these insights, they are experiencing a Now Moment. Up until this point, I have talked primarily about the Now Season. I believe, however, that often life is more about moments than it is about seasons. When we miss moments, we are robbed of the seasons we are living in.

WISDOM KEY

LIFE IS DESIGNED TO CHALLENGE YOU. DON'T LET THE CHALLENGES BECOME YOUR STRUGGLES.

It's like a farmer dreaming about having great crops during harvest season. He talks about having this great season during a particular year, but he doesn't realize that there is an opportunity to purchase seeds at a discounted price or hire some really good workers on a particular day. He continues to dream about having the season, but misses the moments in front of him that could help him start preparing for a great harvest.

So it is with life. Many times, we are excited about our future, the outcome, and even the journey. But life is really about each moment. Remember Sully, the US Airways pilot who landed the commercial aircraft on the Hudson River. He talked about the moment where he had to make a decision. The tower told him to turn around and come back to the airport, but he realized the plane would not make it if he followed those directions. In that moment, he made the decision to land the plane over the water in order to slow it down, and it was the right decision because it saved lives.

Sometimes in a moment, people make a wrong decision—driving a car when drunk, not watching a young child when she or he is by the water or cheating on a spouse. All these decisions in the moment can affect the future in tragic ways.

The point is that whether or not the outcome is bad or good, if we are not aware of those moments and act purposefully, we are not really living life. What moments are you possibly missing that could change your entire season? What are you possibly experiencing that you are ignoring because of the noise of your life?

Hear Beyond the Noise

Life can be noisy whether it's from spiritual, mental, or emotional distractions. We can, however, silence the noise by focusing on one thing instead of all of the things that are going on. In the last chapter, I described how intense my own life can be as an artist, teacher, musician, producer, father, and son. But the way I find success is by focusing on one thing during each moment.

I do multi-task, but only at certain times. For instance, I don't pick up the phone when I am writing a song. I don't plan my travel while visiting my mom. I don't check out who else is in the room when I am having a personal conversation with a person. Quite simply, I have trained myself to live these moments in a purposeful way. I ask myself questions such as: What is the one thing that needs to happen now? What is the one thing in front of me now?

This way of living is not just about the focus of the mind and doing things. It is also about the giving of the heart—your emotion and attitude. We talk about the friends who broke our hearts and hurt our feelings, but what about the friend who is with you now, loving and supporting you? Maybe your heart has been broken in the past, but who is that person who loves you now? Are you giving him or her your moment?

Your Now Moments make up your Now Seasons. When you talk about your Now Season, you're talking about your powerful season. Look at it this way. Your past seasons are dead. They no longer exist. Many people who have been on top are no longer sought after. We don't want to buy their latest albums. We don't want to put them in our latest movies. We don't want them running our country. Their powerful seasons are over.

So you can't look at what you have been, or been through, and think that it's still alive and still powerful. It's not. It's in the past. That season of your life is over, and it's dead. All you can do with dead things is bury them. Of course, you need to acknowledge the past. That's why God gave us the ability to have memories, so that we don't forget where we came from or fail to learn from mistakes. With these memories, we can also smile, laugh, or cry. For instance, you may not move as fast anymore, but you can remember, with joy, the days when you could dance up a storm.

What we have to do in our Now Season, however, is make sure we don't let our past repugnant memories become our Now realities. We can acknowledge a past experience, but we need to move on from it to what is going on now. What is going on now in your life? What is happening around you and in you? Where are you at in this stage? Through this process, you'll begin to discover the richness and value of your Now Season.

If you do this, you will begin to understand that even though you had some great and bad days, amazing opportunities and blessings are waiting for you today, if only you will reach out and grab them. Whatever you focus on becomes the strongest in your life. It becomes the greatest and most powerful thing in that moment.

Recognizing Your Own Now Moment

Everyone has Now Moments, but they may not recognize them. As you read this book, I hope you will see when you either missed a Now Moment or when you took advantage of one. Once you begin to identify a Now Moment, you will be able to begin to move forward.

Let's imagine walking in the woods. If you are like me, being in nature feels very good. It is powerful to be among the trees. One reason is that you are experiencing exactly who you are as a life force on this planet. Like nature, you are always creating, producing, and giving life. You are part of a cosmic system.

The trees release oxygen when they use energy from sunlight to make glucose from carbon dioxide and water. It takes six molecules of carbon dioxide to produce one molecule of glucose by photosynthesis, and six molecules of oxygen are released as a by-product. If trees disappeared and the system stopped working, animals and people would die and life would end.

But because the interconnected systems of oxygen, sun, and plants are always in motion, the world works. We are always on the side of life, not death. We are always moving even if we are sitting still. Each breath is a movement. Your eyes are constantly engaged. Your skin touches the air around you.

Just by being, like that beautiful oak tree in the forest, you are experiencing one of the most extraordinary times of your life. You are alive. You are embracing your Now. Most people don't acknowledge how incredible it is to have a moment, to be in that moment, and to embrace that moment. That moment has great riches because you are in it.

As you read, you are cultivating your mind, heart, and spirit. It's causing something to rise up in you. Some people call it faith. Some people call it hope. Some people call it encouragement. Some people call it inspiration. But whatever it is, it brings forth life to you and causes you to want to live or to give life to others. That's the power of Now.

When I was a child, one of my favorite movies to watch with my brothers and sisters was *The Wizard of Oz*. In that movie, the main character's name is Dorothy, played by the talented actress Judy Garland. In Dorothy's quest to find her path back home, she was led through everything that represented what she didn't have or thought she didn't have—a heart, intelligence, and courage.

All three characters—the Scarecrow, Tin Man, and Lion—exemplified something Dorothy had to discover. Her path and companions allowed her to pull off her blinders so she could have a greater appreciation of who she really was.

So stop looking at what you don't have and start looking at what you do have. That's when you'll notice opportunities you didn't see before, doors you thought were walls and bright paths you thought were dusty roads. The only thing you have to prove is that you have nothing to prove, only a path of experiences that will bring you to a lifetime of purpose.

Now Means More

Here is the beauty of The Now Way of Life. You can have *more* love, strength, and creativity if you seize the moment. The only way you stop feeling and stop having more is when you take your final breath. That in a nutshell is what the Now Season is all about. It's about seizing the moment, living in the moment, and being purposeful in the moment.

Some of my greatest Now Moments were when I was absolutely broke or did not have a shoulder to lean on. It was in those moments that I realized there had to be something I could do. As I began to look around, dig deeper, search more, and cultivate, a whole new crop was planted and became a more awesome season in my life.

At this point, you may reject my theory about the Now, or you may want to stop reading this book. Regardless, the reality is this—life is going on with or without the information in this book. So take that leap of faith. I encourage you to study and embrace Now because it will give you insights, a wealth of knowledge, and a way of looking at your life that I promise is going to help. No matter your stage in life, this knowledge will help you develop new thought patterns that will enhance your life and the lives of people around you.

Do you accept that there is more for you? Can you believe that there is more? Can you begin to understand the possibility of more? Because *Now represents more*—not necessarily more things, but more in life for you to experience, more for you to contribute to, more for you to learn, more opportunities for success and happiness.

That's the question that you have to answer first: *Do you believe there is more?* Because if you do, you will get up right now and do something. You will say, "*Enough is enough!*" Whatever has been, it's over. It's time to create something new and unique. Something that is beyond where you have been and where you are now.

Let me share another story that illustrates this point. As I mentioned before, a major record label signed me back in the day. That's a very big thing for a singer. When you are starting out, you are told that you don't have what it takes to make it on your own. You don't have the skills, ability, or knowledge. I know you have heard the stories about record labels taking advantage of young musicians so that they walk away with very little. That was my case. I knew it was a terrible deal. But when you get that first deal, you take it.

Like so many others, I found myself legally bound to the company that signed me. I wasn't seeing any resources being put toward my success, and they owned my work. I realized that there was no way I could survive and take care of my son with the deal I had. So I found a lawyer who could work with me. We're talking a David and Goliath situation. I began to fight tooth and nail, not only to get out of all deals with the label, but also to regain the masters of my album.

The masters are basically the original rights to a project. Whoever "owns" the master owns the album. Many people think it's the person on the cover, but often that's not the case. The owner is usually the label company. It controls the album and can do whatever it wants. In other words, the company can say, "Hey, listen, we're not pressing, and we're not printing anymore CDs. You won't ever be able to touch it. We're going to put it in a box, put it on the shelf, and you can never have it."

I did not back down. I fought and eventually won. I got out of the deal completely. I was not only able to own my masters, but I was able to take whatever was left in the warehouse and use those extra CDs to jumpstart my touring schedule and career. I took the sales and went back in the studio to make my next album. I couldn't afford a whole band. I couldn't afford a bunch of singers, so I did the background vocals myself with two friends. I had another friend who played the guitar and did production and another who had a studio in a garage. We made it work. We didn't have much time, so we did the entire album in one week. It's still one of my best-selling albums.

This story is an example of seizing the moment in that Now Season to achieve more. I could not worry, wait, complain, or make decisions in fear of "what ifs." It was about just hunkering down and getting it done.

So now I challenge you. Seize the moment. Reach out for more. You can do it, and when you do, you'll feel the release. You'll feel the freedom. You'll feel the excitement. Yes, you will face obstacles; others may doubt you or it may take longer than you think, but I can assure you that if you watch for your Now Moment and act, your reward will be great.

It will have to come from you like most dreams do. I mean, who's dreaming with you when you're sleeping? The dreams come only to you, whatever they are. Dreams are personal, and dreams require the dreamer. So while you may not have that support initially, just move forward, and operate in your Now.

Another piece of advice: It's crucial not to allow negative people into your sphere or space. If you know the story of the garden of Eden from the Bible in the beginning of Genesis, it's not that the devil came in a particularly frightening way or that he came with extravagant promises of luxury. He just made a simple suggestion that caused Adam and Eve to do what God told them not to do; hence, their lives changed dramatically as well as the course of humanity.

Similarly, you may encounter little snide comments, suggestions, and smirks that may push you to abandon your quest. How many people do you know who have given up because of comments from a bitter aunt, a doubting mom, a negative dad, or an envious friend?

Another parable I like is the one about the frogs who were traveling through the woods. Two fell into a deep pit, and the other frogs crowded around and told them there was no hope for them. The two frogs ignored the advice and tried to jump out of the pit. The other frogs continued to tell them to give up because they would never make it out. One frog listened and fell to his death.

The other frog continued to jump even harder although his frog friends told him it was pointless. Finally, he made it out of the pit. . It turns out he was deaf and didn't hear the negative comments. He thought his friends were encouraging him the entire time to keep jumping."

Sometimes we need to be like a deaf frog. We need to stay in a space that allows for positivity about our passions, destinies, dreams, and purpose. This is how we stay enriched in our Now. This is what will cause our atmosphere to stay ignited with great energy, life, and wealth.

Take Away the Safety Net

Why do some kids excel in high school but fail to thrive in college and beyond? Why do popular teenagers sometimes lack friends later in life? One reason is that a safety net protected them so they felt no need to push forward, to press on in difficult times. They never develop that inner voice to push past comfort.

Instead, there's a false belief that life will go on as it always has. But their safe environment will soon become a weight, a chain, and bondage. There will be no demand for real progress and thirst or a drive for more. Their safety net becomes a trapping net. As parents, it's tough not to worry about what your children are getting into and the ultimate impact it will have on their lives. But putting them in too much of a "safe zone" can rob them of their growth.

WISDOM KEY

INNOCULATE YOURSELF WITH THE VACCINE OF FAILURE AND DISAPPOINTMENT

That teenage girl who's always so calculated and not given the room to make mistakes. Or a high school senior boy who has a limitless flow of money to fulfill all his wants but doesn't know how to budget. Or a 16-year-old whose car costs more than his teacher's. Or a daughter who thrives from modeling the latest brands of clothing and throwing big pool parties at the house where she doesn't have real chores.

We create safety nets that make young people walk across the tightrope of life without a consciousness that they could fall and obtain great injury. I'm all for rewarding and giving our children the best that life can offer, but have we helped create adults with no real survival instinct?

We don't have to wash and sanitize everything. Leave some of the dirt so they can have something they can wash off, so that they know it's possible to get dirty—and, even better, to get back clean again.

The same is true of us as adults. Let's look at a different analogy—vaccines. In the case of the flu, a nurse will inject you with the flu virus so that your immune system will be strong enough to combat the virus when it tries to invade your body during the epidemic-scale flu season. Likewise, our lives are injected with vaccines of failures, disappointments, and pain and sufferings that build our defense mechanisms in preparation for us to withstand, conquer, and succeed.

What you are exposed to can become a building block of strength, if you allow it. Some of the most successful men and women today didn't just arrive. They went through tough times—financially, emotionally, health-wise, relationally, and even spiritually. Instead of giving up and throwing in the towel, they took every blow of failure as a stepping-stone to the next gig and the next opportunity to progress.

I Can. I Will. I Am.

We were made to be creative beings. Any time we're not cultivating, creating, and producing fresh things, it takes away from our value and self-worth. We become worthless when we sit back and say, "I can't," and the only reason why many of us say, "I can't" is because we couldn't do it in the past. Our "can't" is a part of our past, but in our present, there is an "I can!"

Now means truly believing *I can*. Now means *I will*. Now means *I am*. Anytime you say you can't do something, you are actually talking in past tense. You can't say you can't do something until you've actually tried to do it. So, if you're talking about something you can't do, that means you're still living in the past. You are still referencing the last time you tried and failed. You may say, "I can't fall in love."

WISDOM KEY

I CAN
I WILL
I AM

But just because you couldn't fall in love back then doesn't mean you can't fall in love today.

You can do it. You can. That's all a part of what it means to live in your Now Moment and Now Season. This has been a vital lesson in my own life. It kept the circle of life within me going. I believe it is so important for every living being to embrace this, whether they are students, a mother, father, spouse, or lover. Make this your mantra: *"I can. I will. I am!"*

Do the Work

One of the things I want you to understand about the power of Now is that it's not what you feel like doing or what you think you should do, but rather what needs to be done. You have to do the work and do it boldly, take a step back and get objective, then move forward with action—even if it means confronting the pain. Can you allow yourself to go beyond your weakness and weariness and get the job done? Can you ask hard questions like "How did this negative situation work for my good?" Or "Why was losing that job best for me?" Or "How did the break-up make my life better?"

As you sift through your distress, you will see the positive side of what you thought was negative. You will find so many nuggets of useful information that will infuse strength into you and release new wisdom, insight, freedom, peace, and an energy that will thrust you further into this new season of your life.

When I pretty much flunked my first semester of college after working so hard to get in, I had to do the work to bounce back, in order to complete my undergraduate degree in the four years I set out to do it in. That meant taking summer classes, courses online, and even courses during the holiday break. But I did the work and finished the goal with the outcome I envisioned. Additionally, when you do the work, it will create a wealth of knowledge that will set you on the path to win.

In the next chapter, I want to talk about understanding your beginnings. Mastering that step in The Now Way of Life will give you the knowledge, insights, and wisdom to achieve happiness and success.

WISDOM KEY

DO THE WORK BOLDLY

In Summary

People yearn for a better life, but yearning doesn't get them anywhere. Instead, you need to do the work to make this your

Now Season. It starts with recognizing Now Moments and living them fully without distraction. I encourage you to grab hold of your Now Moment and understand that you are in it, and then begin to grow in it. You have to want more and realize that settling for good instead of great limits your possibilities. This is completely doable. You just have to do it.

Practice

1. *Learn to recognize your Now Moment. Sit down right now and write exactly what you are doing, why you are doing it, and how you are feeling about what you are doing.*

_____

_____

_____

_____

_____

_____

_____

_____

_____

_____

_____

2. *Repeat.*

_____

_____

_____

_____

_____

_____

3. *Repeat.*

_____

_____

_____

_____

_____

_____

_____

CHAPTER FOUR

UNDERSTANDING YOUR BEGINNING

A man walks into an elephant camp and notices that the only thing keeping the elephants from escaping is a small piece of rope tied to one of their legs. He asks the trainer why they don't use their strength to break the rope and escape. The trainer explains that when the elephants were very young, he used the same rope to hold them. As they grew, they became conditioned to believe they could not break away. They so firmly believe the rope can still hold them that they never even try to break free.

Sometimes, like the elephants, we adopt the belief that things are not possible, that we cannot achieve what we want. That belief often comes from our beginnings. Until we understand our beginnings, we cannot break free from our past and take steps to move forward.

Here's the story of my beginning. I was told by one of my older siblings that they were all so very excited to find out that another baby boy was on the way home from the hospital. Everyone was excited about the twelfth addition to the already large clan of thriving, healthy children.

I was given nicknames and handed off to any of the brothers or sisters who were old enough to hold me. I remember being coached, mentored, and disciplined by no less than nine of my siblings. Can you imagine being corrected and directed by nine different people in addition to your parents? Being disciplined as a child by so many folks left a lasting impression on me, even though they all shared the same values around faith, family, and love.

As I grew up the twelfth of thirteen children, I quickly learned that life does not wait for me, respect my time, or even recognize I exist. Because I had so many to look up to, I was always trying my best to fit in, keep up, and be recognized.

Looking back, I think I was being groomed to face the challenges that would (and will) come later on in life, by the very order in which I was born into my family. You may not realize it, but the very birth order in your family plays a significant role regarding who you are today. Understanding how you fit into your family can provide answers to many questions that you have about yourself.

Your Beginnings Hold Secrets to Many Answers

Even in the Bible, it directs us back to the beginning: *"Before I formed you in the womb I knew you, before you were born I set you apart..." Jeremiah 1:5.* It shows us that God knows and has a plan for each of us before our lives even begin.

You can also infer that your beginning holds mysteries to many answers of why things turned out the way they did. Things like high achievements in your career, challenges in your finances, issues in your relationships, or health complications: these are all results of your beginnings.

When you understand those starting points, you will understand why you think the way you think. Our thoughts are not our own, but rather a combination of our experiences, things that were poured into us, and things we faced earlier in life.

So, the questions become: Have you ever stopped to ask who you were in the beginning? Who was that little girl or little boy? Was he or she shy or outgoing? Was he or she courageous or afraid? Did that little guy or girl feel confident or intimidated about the challenges of life?

Some children will blossom the moment they hit the stage in a play or a recital of a small church poem for Christmas. Others will become courageous leaders on the basketball court, especially when the team is down by just one point and there is less than a minute on the clock in the last quarter. Still others might soar like eagles when tested on their knowledge of math or English literature. These

> WISDOM KEY
>
> CONFRONT AND ACCEPT YOUR BEGINNINGS NO MATTER WHAT

scenarios usually tend to produce by-products and ripple results into the future.

Your beginning can start anywhere, but in these pockets of great energy are clues to the woman or man you are today. As you dig deeper, a light bulb will go off in your head, and you will think, "Ah, that's it. This is where my insecurity is derived from!" Or "Yes, it's music that brings life to me." Or "It was my need to be physically competitive that now brings a desire to push forward."

For us to be powerful, we have to understand where we came from. People may not want to do this because it can be tedious. For some people, it can be extremely intimidating, especially if they are consumed with bad memories. Yes, it is easy to forget where we came from for good reasons. No one wants to revisit a time when they were told what to do or a time they were made to do something they didn't understand. Most people don't want to go back to an era when they were limited in their freedom and no one took their words seriously. After all, you were only a child, and you were treated like one. However, a healthy, balanced, striving adult gains wisdom and gratitude from those moments, even from the times that were dreadful.

Understand, Don't Fix

If you noticed, this chapter is not entitled "Fix Your Beginning," rather "Understand Your Beginning." This is deliberate. So many of us, including myself, beat ourselves up trying to fix, redo, replay, or somehow change the path that has gotten us here. Those of us who are striving for excellence today can fall into a regimen of fighting with the ghosts of yesterday.

The problem with this is that some days we defeat our ghosts, but so many days we lose. When we lose to these old non-existing beings, we lose big. The truth is you don't have the strength to fight something that will never wear down, tire out, or give in, because it doesn't exist until you breathe life back into it.

You see, we don't get to pick or choose how our life begins. We don't choose our parents or siblings, and we don't get to pick our social or economic environment. Think about the children who get adopted by wealthy and famous celebrities. How different would their lives have been if they were left to struggle in some orphanage? Or think about someone who cared for you as a child even though you were not a part of their family. The reality is, whether or not we were rescued or got a hand up, what we do today determines the life we will live out for our tomorrow.

My parents are from the islands of the Bahamas—a very passionate and expressive culture—so it was customary to express ourselves in a passionate manner when we reached our peak of frustration. As I got older, I used that same aggressive tone and attitude when I came across something I didn't like, but that resulted in ruined relationships, friendships, and businesses.

I later came to understand that what took place in my home was not customary in everybody else's home. I'm not saying it's wrong to be expressive; however, my understanding of the beginning shed some light on my attitude and gave me wisdom to be cautious in not being over-the-top. It also gave me an

69

opportunity to understand that not everyone is brought up in a home where they are free to be aggressively expressive. The lesson learned is that sometimes what is okay for you may not be okay for others. When you realize that, you have to be willing to make adjustments.

In order to accept your beginning, you have to first confront it. Some people don't

---

WISDOM KEY

YESTERDAYS NEVER COME AGAIN

---

want to remember, so they hide behind stories that make them look good or feel better about themselves. That's false identification, and a false ID won't get you very far. You cannot associate yourself with fictitious tales and expect to deal with the root of your situation.

Being willing to confront the truth of your situations will bring you to accepting them. Own them. This may involve tough truths, like being abused as a child or flunking out in your final year in high school.

Whatever it was, it was your beginning. You may not have chosen it, but it's how it all started for you. Whether you like it or not, it's all a part of what you've become and where you find yourself today. Some people don't want to remember. Others know, but still have not accepted it. Whatever the case, until you come to that point of confronting and accepting, growth and healing will not take place.

Improving Your Future

Many of us live from year to year, hauling unresolved issues and casting rods of self-fulfilling prophecies into our future. We say, "It is what it is" or "I will never be good enough." Then we wonder why life is still the same or worse.

I remember thinking as a child that life was so vast and so incredibly big. I thought that I could have everything I saw on television or dreamed about. What's funny about our beginning is that while we're there, we don't foresee sad or disappointing endings. No one thinks, "I'm going to grow up and have someone I love betray me." No one thinks, "I will face prejudice from people who don't even know me because of the color of my skin, weight, or culture." No one thinks, "I will fail more times than I will succeed." No, we just consider the beginning as a place of endless good possibilities. And then we give it away.

Understanding my beginning helped me to realize that on paper I was not supposed to win. I wasn't qualified to achieve much. I wasn't the brightest kid in the classroom. I didn't have the skill or ability of a star athlete. In my circle of influence, there were no great leaders or entrepreneurs. There were no *American Idol* winners that started off as-no name singers and catapulted into stardom overnight. I thought I was destined to work nine-to-five and never find financial security.

I had to find the zeal, the will, and the power to say, "I want more than this! I want to go further than where I am." Many of the greats throughout history had very similar moments in life where they decided to take a problem and turn it into purpose.

Albert Einstein didn't have the best childhood. In fact, many people thought he was just average at best. He didn't speak for the first three years of his life, and once he made it to elementary school, many of his teachers thought he was just lazy and wouldn't make anything of himself. He always received good marks, but his head was always in the clouds, conjuring up abstract questions people couldn't understand. He, however, kept thinking and eventually developed the theory of relativity, which many of us still can't wrap our heads around.

> WISDOM KEY
>
> THE PEOPLE THAT CAN'T <u>GROW</u> WITH YOU, CAN'T <u>GO</u> WITH YOU

Benjamin Franklin's parents could only afford to keep him in school until his tenth birthday. But that didn't stop this great man from pursuing his education. He taught himself through voracious reading and eventually went on to invent the lightning rod and bifocals. Today, he's one of this great nation's Founding Fathers.

Even tragic childhoods can birth great leaders, entrepreneurs, and extraordinary parents. I actually believe that those who have less in the beginning have the greatest possibility of ending up with the most in the end because they are forced to have imagination. They have to dream it up because it isn't within their reach.

For them, there's no pool in the backyard or three meals each day. There is no loving father or doting mother to come home to after school. For many, it is about waking up on their own, finding what they can to eat, and walking miles to get to school to face a group of people who may or may not like them.

It doesn't matter how you start, but what you do with where you are in that moment. Your beginning may be rocky, but it could end in great wealth and accomplishments. You need to know that "*weeping may endure for a night, but joy comes in the morning.*" *Psalm 30:5.* You just have to hang in there.

Who You Are

Who were you before you became you? Before situations and people told you who to be? Before you met the bitter you, the stagnant you, the losing you, or the unstable you? What pushed you to where you are today?

All human beings start with an innate, primitive determination and a clean slate. These change as they experience life's challenges. You can see this in babies who will not stop crying until they get something to eat. They will continue to wail until they get what they want, no matter how dry their throats are or how tired their bodies feel.

We are all born with the need to accomplish and achieve, but unfortunately, our accumulated misfortunes in life can distort this desire. You may feel you don't fit in or will never make it. Maybe someone told you you're not beautiful. Perhaps a teacher reduced your self-esteem by telling you that you wouldn't amount to anything. Or it could be the humiliating words of your coach, "You don't have what it takes to make the team."

The bottom line is your outcome and success are not based on what people told you, but what you decide today and what you choose to tell yourself. There are layers that can get in the way of the mirror, but you can pull back those layers so you can get to your true reflection.

Do you remember the story of the ugly duckling that became a beautiful swan? The baby swan was mocked, laughed at and rejected because she didn't look, walk, or quack like the ducks that she grew up with. Even though she was born a swan and already had that genetic makeup of beauty, the only reference the swan had was that of the ducklings. Because there was no resemblance, she felt ugly and didn't feel like she fit in.

Many people walk through life with that same ugly duckling syndrome, having that feeling of not fitting in and not having a place or a voice in this world. The reality is that you have not found your space and you have not found your purpose.

Discovering your purpose and finding your space comes from using the right language when you talk about yourself. You need to accept what you have and use it to its fullest potential. For example, it's not okay to say, "I'm not educated," or "I don't know enough." By saying those words, you are casting a rod of limitation into your future by actually saying, "That's where I'm always going to always be; that's my level or my limit!"

What's really happening here is you are missing your moment of developing the "current you" and preventing yourself from moving forward to the "future you," with the potential to be more educated and wiser. Instead, talk about yourself in this way: "I may not be as educated as I want to be, but that will not stop me from moving forward. I will make the choice to use whatever education I have to its fullest potential, and eventually I'll get to the level I desire."

I once saw two old men fighting over a basketball game. It got so heated that they almost got physical. I was with one of my older brothers and said to him, "Wow, can you believe those old men are about to physically fight over something so small and irrelevant?"

My brother's response was both simple and profound, "Little brother, stupid people don't become smart when they get older. They just become old stupid people."

I actually laughed, but then realized in that moment that I better keep studying, reading, and growing because I didn't want to become another "old stupid person." My moment of insight was realizing that time doesn't stop for anyone. It will move, but in order to gain ground and achieve purpose, you have to move with it.

Beginnings are Not Just About Childhood

Your beginning is not just linked to your childhood; it could start at any point as you grow and experience life. For instance, your current situation could be directly connected to something you encountered six months, five years, or even ten years ago.

Take your health, for example. If you pay attention, you will notice the questions a doctor asks concerning a chronic or an acute condition. Most of the time, the doctor will go to your recent medical history and ask questions about your current habits of eating, drinking, and your overall lifestyle. As your doctor probes, he or she gains an understanding to give you a proper diagnosis of why you are facing health issues.

The same is true about behavior. There are people who are afraid because of a loss earlier in life, and there are people who deal with a constant need to achieve or succeed because of an early encounter. If your mother suffered from depression, then you may discover you have similar feelings. What you learn from her condition can give you the insight to take actions so you do not follow that path.

Don't Forget Where You Came From

Think about the first generation of immigrants. Usually that generation is known to have accomplished more than their descendants. Why? Because there was a real sense of urgency, knowing where they came from but understanding that there is no staying there.

This is why you will sometimes hear older people say, "Don't forget where you came from." This is not about residing in the past, but rather perceiving that all of your past has led you here. When you get it, you will see that there is a sense of responsibility that must be taken on: "I am standing on the shoulders of greatness—of my great-great-grandmother, my great-great-uncle, and my great-great-grandfather."

Somebody paid the price so that you could have this jumping-off point. Even if it isn't as high, it's still a jumping-off point that your ancestors didn't have. It's in this concept that we begin to understand that we can then take the failures, upsets, losses, wins, and achievements and fasten them into a totality that helps us understand that it was all meant to be from the beginning.

We all have different family beginnings. Some of us are comfortable with them; others feel alienated or distressed in their God-given families. The truth is that it doesn't matter if you were adopted, born into a good family, or had no family at all. What I want you to know is that you matter, you made it, and you can move beyond where you are right now. That no matter what it looked like in the beginning, you have the power to change it now.

Love the Moments that Bring Joy

One of my cherished moments was being in my parents' backyard when the weather went from sunny and cheerful to gray and rainy. Friends, siblings, and other family members would be sitting, leaning, or standing as music from a cassette player competed with the loud laughter and chattering from people catching up or making fun of each other. In every corner of that space, someone was present.

But that would change when gray clouds started rolling in. Everyone hastened to get in the house, just so the drizzling rain wouldn't catch them. I took it all in. That was my moment. My space that was once limited because of people and noise now was occupied only by me, the big fluffy gray clouds, drizzles of rain smaller than teardrops, and the soft whistling wind.

It was the only time that I would have the backyard to myself—an uninterrupted space where I would dream of being the only child in the house with a big backyard.

Other special moments were private times with my dad when we were going somewhere for ministry or church. On one of our trips, I remember sitting behind him in the van and asking, "Dad, do you think I'm a good singer?" In his baritone voice he responded, "Yes, of course."

I was awestruck, hearing that from him. This somber island man, who had, in his later years, always had a serious demeanor. He was always about business, never played the radio, and didn't give many compliments. So, when Dad told me that, it meant a lot to me, and I cherished that moment.

We sometimes overlook those special instances because we've had a lot more challenging times. But they are there, even if they never came from your home. It may have come from a bus driver, a school teacher, the old lady next door who always gave you a slice of cake, a church member, a pastor, or even a stranger who pointed you in the right direction.

If you pause, think, and dig for them, you will find those moments in your beginning. The reason you want to find them is to gain strength from them, to get an opportunity to say, "*Some-*

one did care in the beginning season of my life," and know that God also cared by sending that person to you.

Cherish What Made You Different

We have to interact with people at work and in our community. Until we gain the wisdom we need from understanding our beginnings, we will not be able to understand others and help them in the same manner we may have helped ourselves. It is only then that you will be able to see the difference between a manipulated mind-set of beliefs and what is really truth and reality.

Your co-workers, for example, may be giving you the manifestation of anger, but if you look a little deeper, it's coming from a place of hurt because of what they've been exposed to. And because you have dealt with that type of hurt and have graduated from it, you are able to see beyond the walls of anger, understand, help, and connect with that person despite their lashing out.

We often disregard the phrase that a person becomes a product of his or her environment, but there's much truth to it. Your environment could be fashioned with two loving parents who are financially stable, while another person's environment may consist of a struggling single mother. Each environment becomes the beginning of many things that will be passed on to the child.

Psychological research studies have shown some key differences in the characteristics between the first, middle, and last children. Additionally, cultural differences and family traditions play a big role in a person's way of doing things. Knowing these things will also give you the advantage needed to overcome current challenges with the people around you more quickly.

Let me tell you what weekly dinner times with my family were like for me growing up. On Sunday's there were always cafeteria-style pots with four or five chickens being baked at once and a huge pot of rice. As an adult, I assumed that everyone grew up with big pots and lots of rice, only to realize that a lot of people had their own traditions where they ate out with their families or cooked smaller portions.

Our Christmases were unlike others, very loud with music and over the top with resounding laughter and conversations among forty or fifty family members sitting around the Christmas tree. Countless pieces of gift-wrapping paper would layer the floor from the many gifts we unwrapped, so we would roll up those papers like snowballs and throw them at each other, which became our annual Christmas Paper-Fight every year.

This started when we were very small children and, to this day, our own children do the same. Here again, I thought this happened in every household, only to realize this was something unique to only a few families that I have come across. We still have that same annual Christmas Paper-Fight every year and we have passed it on to the grandchildren now.

Don't Get Stuck in the Past

Oftentimes, the older we get, the more we want to go back to what we were used to as a child—the simple life of walking to the store two blocks from the house or having only familiar faces in your neighborhood. Just because something was great in the past or you had this awesome one-time experience before doesn't mean that is how the rest of your life should be lived or how it will turn out.

Don't make the same mistake as the little boy who found the copper penny while walking down the street one day. He was so excited that he found money. This experience led him to spend the rest of his days walking with his head down, with eyes wide open, looking for treasures. During his lifetime he found 296 pennies, forty-eight nickels, nineteen dimes, sixteen quarters, two half dollars, and one crinkled dollar bill. He collected a grand total of $13.26.

He got money for nothing, except that he missed the breathless beauty of 31,369 sunsets, the colorful splendor of 157 rainbows, and the fiery beauty of hundreds of maples nipped by autumn's frost. He never saw white clouds drifting across blue skies, shifting into various wondrous formations. Birds flying, sun shining, and the smiles of a thousand passing people were not a part of his memory.

Learn from Pain

Pain, in my opinion, is often a powerful driver of success, and we can learn from those whose pain has made them strong. The level of pain a person goes through can determine how strong that person can become—like those who endured the civil rights movement. Also, think about the many Jewish people who had

81

to face discrimination, and those that went through the Holocaust. There are so many other issues that people have dealt with that caused them pain, yet they still had a reason to want to live and survive. The fact that they still held on proved that these are extremely successful people.

As I have said before, success is not about money; it's about enduring tough times yet staying with it. Having the ability to say, "I made it," and "I'm making it," is directly tied to your Now. The reality is: if I were able to be successful despite my past struggles and challenges, then certainly I can and will be successful through my current challenges and struggles.

So, you do have to love and embrace your great moments in your beginning, but you also have to gain from your painful moments, even if they are very sensitive. If you were a victim of child abuse, you need to understand that it wasn't your fault; you are not responsible for the bad things that people did to you.

Psychologists tell us that a person's mind is fully developed by the time they are three years old. Whatever experience he or she has from that point on, you are still dealing with the same person. You want to embrace these things because they help you to understand how your mind is working now and how you perceive things as an adult.

In many ways, as adults we still think as children. It's not like something just says, "Ok, it's time to convert from a pre-teen to a teenager," and then you have a teenage mind. It's not like something just clicks in your mind and instantly revamps you from a teenager to an adult. It doesn't just switch. Time and experiences, however, will bring about development, but it's the same mind going through different stages. If your now-adult mind is not transformed by understanding through life-developing processes, then you could look at an abusive situation and think that you brought that on yourself because you thought you were in control as an independent person when in fact you, the then child, were not in control at all.

There are so many things embedded in us that didn't appear overnight—laziness, bitterness, and anger. There are many people who don't know when they're getting angry or understand why they respond to others aggressively. They never identified with their beginnings to learn that these are things they've picked up along the way, things that might have been associated with pains they experienced. Nevertheless, all you have is this perfect moment, this perfect season called "Right Now," and it says that you can learn from it all and gain from it all. I hope you're ready because your best days are still ahead of you.

Billionaire television host and producer Oprah Winfrey is a prime example of how life's tragedies can become life's triumphs. Her childhood years were not what anyone would desire; yet they propelled her to greatness and molded her heart with empathy toward people who currently are struggling.

As a young child under the care of her grandmother, she had to deal with the absence of both of her parents. At age nine, she was raped by a close family member who was entrusted to keep an eye on her. She constantly experienced occurrences of sexual molestation and physical abuse by a family friend and an uncle. At age 14, Oprah became pregnant and gave birth to her son, who died two weeks later.

Those experiences should have broken her. But it actually became the better part of her as she learned and grew from her struggles. As she said during an interview, "Everyone is looking for validation. I know what it feels like to not be wanted...you can use it as a stepping stone to build great empathy for people." And that's what she did. She used her struggles as stepping stones, and they got her to where she is today.

Today Oprah Winfrey is an iconic leader who has received numerous honors that include the most prestigious awards and highest industry acknowledgments. She has beaten the odds, not only as a woman and a woman of color, but also as one who prevailed through a rough childhood. She exemplifies a person who did not let herself get stuck in the past, but chose to live each Now Season boldly. In the next chapter, I am going to talk with you about ways to get unstuck so you can thrive in the Now.

In Summary

Accept your beginnings as they are and not how you wanted them to be. In order to accept your beginning, you have to first confront it. Being willing to confront the truth of your situations will bring you to accepting them. After you have faced them, seen them and heard them, then accept them.

This may involve tough truths like child abuse or flunking out in your final year in high school and not graduating. Whatever it was, it was your beginning. You may not have chosen it, but it's how it all started for you. Whether you like it or not, it's all a part of what you've become and where you find yourself to-day. Until you come to that point of confronting and accepting, growth and healing will not take place.

Practice

1. *As you take this journey of understanding your beginning, write about it and share your experiences as a child. Do this exercise with people who are not from your upbringing. When you share it among those with like experiences, you are just affirming each other. But with people from different backgrounds, you will bring light to them, and they will shed new light on your situation. As you start talking, it will help you to understand the differences and the uniqueness of what you have. When that begins to unfold itself, it's like an onion as you start peeling back layers. You'll realize that at the core of who you are, there are all these different experiences—good, bad, and indifferent—but they all affect how you move in your Now Moments.*

---

2. *Listen carefully to these statements. Think, pray, and express yourself about them. Draw, sing, or write—whatever feels best to you.*

- *Accept your beginnings as they are, not how you want them to be.*

- *If you don't understand the beginning, it is difficult to overcome current challenges.*

- *Your beginning may be rocky, but you could achieve great wealth and accomplishment.*

- *You don't have to fix your past. You just need to have a healthy and balanced awareness of it.*

- *When you understand your beginnings, you gain the wisdom to help identify with others and form a fellowship.*

_____

_____

_____

_____

_____

_____

_____

_____

_____

_____

_____

_____

_____

_____

_____

_____

_____

_____

_____

_____

_____

_____

CHAPTER FIVE

GETTING UNSTUCK

A wise man was visited by scores of people complaining about the same problems every time they sought his counsel. One day he told them a joke, and everyone roared with laughter. A few minutes later, he told them the same joke and only a few people laughed. Then he told the same joke for a third time, and no one even cracked a smile. "Ah," he said, "you can't laugh at the same joke over and over. So why are you always crying about the same problem?"

Many of us live in a place where we just don't seem able to get unstuck. Our marriages seem to be a repeat of the same arguments. Our jobs leave us bored and unhappy. Our children get into constant trouble. Our financial situation is always precarious. We cry again and again about the same problem.

We can even get stuck in our own success—like the story I told you about moving from Florida to California. I appeared to be successful. I had cars, a house, and a stable job. But I was uncomfortable with "just enough." I felt restless and unfulfilled because I knew there was more. So how do you get unstuck so you can thrive in your Now Season? I have some recommendations.

Living with Hope

One way to get unstuck is to live with hope in mind. Hope means possibilities. You wake up each day knowing that there are fresh possibilities in every day, in each moment, and in every season of your life. Life will then become a never-ending journey of discovery.

Think of it like a scavenger hunt where you find different clues placed along the way. You have a chance to discover those things that connect you to the greater purpose of your life. But the key to being a good scavenger is searching and digging as you are driven to find the next clue and how you can use it.

A passage in the Bible is relevant to this discussion: *"Blessed are those who hunger and thirst for righteousness, for they will be filled" (Matthew 5:6).* So I ask: What are you hungry for, and what are you thirsty for?

One way to keep from getting stuck is to stay thirsty and hungry. Many people equate being hungry and thirsty to passion or owning things. I hear, "I'm not passionate about anything." Or "I don't care about a lot of stuff." Or, "I don't know what I'm connected to." Essentially, they talk as if they are full. If you are full, then no matter how tantalizing the food is, you are not going to eat it.

To be honest, you don't have to be passionate about anything. You don't have to be excited about anything. You just have to be hungry and desperate enough. We don't know what is going to happen today, but we can approach it with wonder and hope. I can't tell you how many times I said, "I'm just going to go to the beach," and it became an extraordinary day. Or "I'm just going to take this trip," and it turned out to be one of the best adventures in my life.

How many times have we been invited to a party that we didn't want to go to because we didn't know anybody, didn't feel like getting dressed, or were tucked in a warm bed? Then we went anyway and had the best time of our lives. Maybe we met the love of our life. Maybe we met our business partners or made incredible connections that opened all kinds of doors. And it didn't happen because we were passionate about the party.

So, you don't have to be connected or passionate about anything—you just need to be open to the unknown. Be excited about the possibility of possibilities. If you do that, then opportunities are not lost.

Detach from the Past

Another way to get unstuck is to let go of your past. Some people have a tendency of holding past situations over your head, and you may also do it to yourself— particularly if you stay in a place that always reminds you of the past, a place that makes you feel like a failure or worse. The truth is that season is over and that situation is done.

If you grew up in poverty, you don't have to live in poverty today. If you mishandled your finances, you don't have to continue to do so. If you had an opportunity to start a business and it didn't go well, that doesn't necessarily mean you are a bad businessperson. You can try again, having learned from your mistakes.

Many well-known people were considered failures at some point in their lives. People like Henry Kroger, J. C. Penney, and Sam Walton, each of whom built shopping empires. People like Abraham Lincoln, who, after losing seven political elections and appointments, became one of this nation's greatest leaders. Even though they failed in their beginnings, they still had the tenacity to get back up. Their hope and belief in their dream drove them to search and act on the next thing, despite what they had been through.

I meet people all the time who have experienced this truth. They may not have started major companies or won political offices, but through perseverance and optimism they have put failure behind, learned from it and finally achieved success. This is how I also lived my life. It is how I overcame a broken heart. It is how I overcame failed relationships. It is how I have overcome not only my own mistakes but the injuries done to me by others as well.

Success is about failing and getting back up. You say to yourself: "That was a rock or crack in the sidewalk, so, I am going to watch more carefully." Or, "That coffee table is a little longer than I thought when I bumped my knee; I'm going to walk with caution the next time." You wouldn't just throw out the coffee table; you'll just walk a little wider and keep it moving.

Wisdom, Knowledge, and Understanding

Getting unstuck is grounded in wisdom, knowledge, and understanding. Wisdom is something that comes from experiences that are developed through understandingThe book of Proverbs tells us about a house that is standing on these three principles. *Through wisdom is an house builded; and by understanding it is established: And by knowledge shall the chambers be filled with all precious and pleasant riches. A wise man is strong; yea, a man of knowledge increaseth strength. For by wise counsel thou shalt make thy war: and in multitude of counsellors there is safety. Proverbs 24:3-6*

This means that your life is held together by the principles of wisdom, knowledge, and understanding. If knowledge is the information, then understanding is the action of it, and wisdom is the experience gained from it.

We have already discussed how memory allows us to access our past and hopefully gain wisdom through good and bad experiences. Our past can help us make wise choices for the future. We don't want to repeat

WISDOM KEY

OPPORTUNITIES ARE NOT LOST- SOMEONE ELSE JUST TAKES THEM

mistakes, so understanding our personal history helps us to exercise wisdom. It puts us in a better position to avoid choices that bring regrets or result in difficult circumstances the next time something similar pops up.

I remember a time when the economy was booming. Obtaining a loan to purchase properties was fairly easy. Proving your income was as simple as writing up a profit and loss statement and presenting it to the bank. People were loaned hundreds of thousands of dollars to invest in real estate for homes or businesses.

In the middle of this real estate boom, I was purchasing quite a few properties when the bubble burst, so I got stuck with properties in foreclosure. Thankfully, I didn't lose a lot, but I did go through some hardship. Today I still like to invest in properties, but because of the experience I had, I now know to be more modest in how much I take on in a given period of time.

Often when we encounter new situations or opportunities, we don't have enough of the right knowledge. While we might make the best decisions we can make in that Now Moment, the result might not be all we expected. But with experience and learning, we can make a better decision when similar opportunities arise.

WISDOM KEY

DON'T ALLOW YOUR CIRCUMSTANCES TO MAKE YOU A <u>BITTER PERSON</u>, ALLOW THEM TO MAKE YOU A <u>BETTER PERSON</u>

One caution: Be careful about making false assumptions. Even if a situation looks familiar, it's probably not the same, so think of it as a new challenge.

That's how you don't get stuck. That's how you don't walk into a new relationship treating it like the old one. Yes, there might be some similarities in the person you are dating, but that's a different person. You have to use opportunities to deal with that person in his or her own unique way. The same is true for businesses, careers, and every-day choices. You cannot allow what you've been through to dictate who you are or who you should be.

You have the right to the emotions of what you've been through, but you should not become what you've gone through. What you've gone through should bring about key lessons and wisdom. It should bring about directions on how to move forward for your future, and where your life will go from this point. But it certainly should not turn you into your experience.

We have all met someone who has allowed his or her past experiences to determine current behavior, often to their disadvantage. A father has a rebellious child who does not listen, so he becomes rigid in his treatment of all his other children. A woman's ex-husband cheated on her, so she watches her current husband like a hawk, even violating his privacy. A business partner cheats a man, so he approaches all other dealings with unwarranted suspicion.

Knowledge and Opportunity

Knowledge comes from experiences of all kinds, including lectures from parents, school lessons, the news, projects at work, interactions with friends, travel, social media—even a good book like the one you're reading now. It's impossible to succeed in life without knowledge. People perish for lack of knowledge. Opportunities are missed. Purpose is restrained. Life withers away. The simple truth is that when you have knowledge, you have opportunity.

Let me explain it this way. Information is knowledge, and with knowledge you can open doors that lead to opportunity—a favorable situation or chance for advancement. These doors of opportunities are all around you. For a variety of reasons, you may not be aware of them, but once you are, you will have a choice: open the door or turn away. Remember, you are just one doorknob turn away from your next level of success, wealth, and healthy living.

Where a lot of people fail is when they don't understand the wealth of knowledge that they have learned from the situations they've been through. Most of us just want to see each experience as just an experience, but all experiences hold lessons.

> ### WISDOM KEY
>
> WE STAND <u>ON</u> OUR PAST, BUT WE DON'T STAND <u>IN</u> OUR PAST

I had to be treated like an outcast in order to learn that people are different everywhere you go. This knowledge taught me how to approach each situation uniquely. Who knew that my being rejected and treated differently could give me the information I needed to develop into the person I am today?

When reflecting on your experiences, ask yourself questions such as these: *How was I strengthened from this adversity? What security did I gain from that struggle? What pulled me up out of that desolate place?*

Listen for the answers objectively. When they come, embrace them and apply the knowledge to your current situation, whether it is finances, relationships, health, or some other troubling issue. You will then gain an even greater understanding of how to work it to your benefit.

Working on Your Life Muscles

When people work out in a gym, they don't necessarily see the ripping and growth of their muscles while pumping weights. Instead, they are focused on techniques of motion and breathing.

The result after a period of time will be a fit physique that represents the knowledge they applied while in the heat and sweat of the workouts. They don't want to stop during the reps or the climb of the run because they have learned that to get the results they want, they have to finish the full workout process.

Such is life. You won't see the lessons in the midst of a breakup or in a financial crisis. You won't see the foundation for growth that was created from being fired from your job with your mortgage, car loan, and a demanding spouse staring you in the face. You won't get it when emotions are flaring like fireworks, pressure is pushing you to the edge, and survival mode kicks in.

You may have the information and knowledge, but you won't have the understanding then. But as you venture into similar experiences in your Now Season, that understanding will come to you, and you will get much better results the next time you are faced with similar dilemmas

It's one thing to have information; it's another for you to apply it while going through the situation. The reason is that, many times, we don't actually realize what we are going through while going through it. How can you apply what you know about surviving a breakup, when you didn't know your relationship was in danger?

You remember the expression, "Hindsight is 20/20?" It's easier to see something after you've gone through it; understanding is the thing you get after you've gained knowledge from your experiences.

Common sense will tell you that if you do things a certain way, you are going to get a certain result. Unfortunately, common sense is not that common during some tragedies and disappointments in life. Wisdom requires memory, knowledge, and a healthy balance to one of the most important questions in everyday life: *What do I want the outcome to be?* Wisdom comes into play when the information that is received is understood and then acted upon without going through the same bad experience again and again.

Imperfection: The New Perfection

Let me leave you with one last thought on how to get unstuck: Embrace imperfection. It is a shame that people are trapped in a web of lies about what is perfect. We've heard beautiful people say that they don't feel pretty, and we wonder, "What in the world are they talking about?" We know of people who suffered from bulimia or anorexia because of the pressure of thinking they were overweight.

We use false information about who we are and what we were meant to be. We hold up a false standard of perfection. We develop a sense of disconnect and self-hate because we think we are failing against this false measure. This results in a self-hate that can even lead to suicide and depression.

Here's the truth. Imperfection is not a bad thing. In fact, imperfection is the new perfection. It should be embraced as the soil of creativity, a fertilizer for success, and a seed that spurs the desire to achieve. Sometimes life's imperfections are God's way of saying, "You're not done yet." There is more living, achieving, and success yet to be conquered. It just may be that if you reach that place you think is "perfect," your life might be done.

I hope by this point you have a clear idea that getting unstuck is something you can begin today. One reason people are stuck is that they are not truly living through their Now Moments and Now Seasons. They avoid, quit, or simply do not want to do the work required. In the next chapter, I will discuss strategies you can take to live through life's challenges.

In Summary

Getting unstuck begins with hope. You have to believe that more and better things will be in your future. This does not mean sitting back and doing nothing. Rather, it means taking information and turning it into knowledge and wisdom. It means learning from mistakes but not calling yourself a mistake.

⸎

Practice

Grab a piece of paper, find a quiet room, and answer these two important questions:

   1. What are you hungry and thirsty for in your life?

_____

_____

_____

_____

_____

_____

_____

_____

_____

2. *What is keeping you stuck from moving on?*

_____

_____

_____

_____

_____

_____

_____

_____

_____

_____

_____

_____

_____

CHAPTER SIX

LIVING THROUGH IT

Many people feel like they have what it takes to make it, yet they are not willing to go through what it takes to get it. Even worse, few actually learn from what they have been through. Living through something is different from going through something. Living through means to continue to advance in life while you go through a tough situation. Even if you are faced with a sudden death in the family or financial hardship, you continue the journey of life and don't feel the need to go into a season of giving up on who you are and what you were meant to be.

They say the sun shines brightest after the darkest storm. That, not only is there the potential for better things, but you become better for having lived through it. I personally believe that I became more humble and compassionate because of the trials I endured. When you persevere through different seasons of difficulty, it may get bitter before it becomes better, but it can still be the best thing for you and for your growth.

Unfortunately, many people get through tough times by quitting and walking away. I can relate to that. There have been many days when I felt that way about my career. Yet even though I wanted to give up, I learned that if I just stick it out as I go through each circumstance, another bigger, better, and stronger project will be born. This is what happened when I stayed in college and when I moved to California. And this is what is happening as I take the message of The Now Way of Living around the world.

It's easy to fall into a pity party over a situation that seems impossible to overcome. But my question to you is: Will you learn how to thrive through adversity and experience the wealth that victory can bring when you chose to live through it, or will you give up?

The Chef and His Daughter

There was a young woman who felt her life was miserable. She complained to her father about the continuous struggles she faced. Despondent, she really did not know if she could go on. Her father was a chef, and he took her back to the kitchen where he started boiling three pots of water.

In one pot, he placed potatoes. Eggs went into the second pot. Ground coffee beans were added to the third. After twenty minutes he turned off the burners and put the potatoes into one bowl, the hard-boiled eggs into a second, and poured the coffee into a cup. "What do you see?" he asked his daughter.

She sighed and answered, "Potatoes, eggs, and coffee."

"Please touch the potato and egg and drink the coffee," he said.

She did so, asking him, "What does this have to do with my miserable life?"

The chef explained that the potatoes, the eggs, and coffee beans each faced the same adversity—boiling water. Yet each reacted differently.

The potato went from strong and hard to soft and crumbling. The egg started out fragile and became hard. The ground coffee beans actually changed the water and became something new. "Which one are you, my daughter? Are you a potato, egg, or coffee?" he asked.

WISDOM KEY

IT'S IN OUR FAILURE THAT GREATNESS IS DEVELOPED

So what are you? Do you become soft and crumbling like the potato? Do you become hard when faced with challenges like the egg? Or do you instill change in yourself and the world around you like the ground coffee beans?

How we choose to live life—both in good and bad times—defines who we are as people. Two people can experience a tragedy in their lives and react in totally different ways. One may curl up and live the rest of their life in emotional and physical pain. The other overcomes tragedy like a phoenix rising. I've seen this over and over again with people I talk with.

A child faces a life-threatening illness. One parent flees, and the other buckles down and becomes a fearless advocate. A plant closes, and hundreds lose their jobs. Some are crushed and live a life dependent on government or family handouts. Others rebuild, find new careers, and even start their own companies.

Life is always in motion, and things will always happen to us and around us. If we choose to react by turning struggles into opportunities, this will define us as individuals and set profound examples for our children and their generation.

Dealing with Process

There's an expression I like a lot, "God does not close a door without opening another one." I'm sure you've heard that before. But here's the version I think that is more realistic about life: "God does not close a door without opening another one, but the hallway sure can be hell."

> WISDOM KEY
>
> YOU CAN TELL HOW SUCCESSFUL YOU ARE BY THE SIZE OF THE PROBLEMS YOU'RE FACING

The hallway, path, or process, while you are in your Now Season, can be rough. Looking back on my career, the difficulty was enduring the process, whether it was making music and movies or transitioning between being a recording artist, a speaker, an actor, and a producer. As I kept moving on, I found out how difficult going through things can be and that rough times always come before reaching the goal.

It is human nature to try to find an easy way out or through a process. Personally, I discovered that if I was getting too comfortable, I probably was missing something. The majority of the times when we are going through something, the reason why it becomes extremely tough is because of our natural instinct to look for comfort. But that's not how you live successfully through changing seasons. In life, you don't look to be comfortable. You look to be purposeful.

Finding comfort during a difficult situation may get you temporary gain, but it may also cause permanent damage to the outcome. Can you imagine what would happen if an expecting mother self-induced labor at twenty-eight weeks only because she could no longer deal with the discomfort her body was going through? Undoubtedly, it would be a relief to her body; however, there would be a very slim chance that the child would live or not develop long-term disabilities. Any mother would rather have a healthy child with mature organs, better breathing capability, and more strength for feeding, which comes from a full-term pregnancy.

So it is with our problematic processes. We all would rather find a quick or easy way through it, but the end product might not be what we had hoped for. This is why you don't look at what is easy; instead, you look at what will bring completion. And if the right way means it's going to be a little harder, longer, or more challenging, then go ahead and walk through the harder process because in the end it's going to benefit you in a better way.

Practicing Endurance

Some people don't live through their processes, but they are dormant until the process is over. This is simply going through the motions—there's no care, no belief that things will work out, no fight, and no involvement in their own battles. There is no endurance.

The quality of endurance is the power of withstanding hardship or stress. It literally means to persevere or to continue in existence. Just because you are in tough times, it doesn't mean that you are supposed to just take it. Yet, I've seen this happen so many times. I've witnessed people who had major catastrophes with their finances, family, and relationships, and they did nothing. Too many think, "There's nothing else I can do." But have we done our best? As Duke Ellington once said, "A problem is a chance for you to do your best."

Doing nothing generally means quitting. Of course, quitting is an option, one that I did many times when I was in the college band. This made me a professional quitter—leaving that group five times in four years. But I came back every time, and I practiced endurance even though I didn't want to. And as I matured, I realized that quitting should never be an option for me as I live in my Now Season.

Remember, quitting and doing nothing are both conscious choices, but the outcome of either will affect you negatively in more ways than you can imagine. So instead of saying, "I have a right to just quit," try these words instead: "In spite of this difficulty, I'm going to persevere and have a better outcome. Instead of just going through the motions, I'm going to fight to become better because of it."

"Why?" Versus "How?"

Gaining from a painful situation can provide revelations and lead us to uncover hidden truths about ourselves. But we have to be careful not to focus on the wrong questions so we won't go in the wrong direction. We are derailed by questions like "Why did I have this death in my family? Why was I diagnosed with this sickness? Why did I lose my job when the company downsized?"

It's very natural to ask "why" when uncertainty hits, and we want to know the mysteries behind our misfortunes. But it negatively affects what we will gain from our difficult situations. The reality is that sometimes we won't know the answers why. In fact, the majority of the time the answers to "why" never come. If they do, they can mislead, distract, or even cripple us, which keeps us bound to our past so we never experience the power of Now.

On the contrary, we should ask the very important question of "how." "How am I supposed to go through this situation in my life? How do I position myself in the midst of it? How can I learn to make the necessary changes? How can I use this opportunity to learn and gain understanding?"

The question of "how" will help you move forward as opposed to the question of "why," which can hold you in the past.

Imagine you are used to being praised for your personality and job performance. Then you move to a new job where people are critical of you. You might put up resistance or blame the new company and boss because you don't know or agree with the "why." This will only make it more difficult for you to navigate through the new job. Instead, you should ask how you can improve and use the criticism to find success and growth.

When you are in a financial crisis, ask the question, "How do I get out of this?" It is a question that could lead you to become self-sufficient. The "how" can point you in the right direction of finding the entrepreneur in you.

You may never find the reason why you go through tough times; however, finding an interpretation can be helpful, because what you interpret may be a hidden lesson. In light of this, you can also ask yourself, "How am I supposed to interpret this? How am I supposed to understand this? What is it that I'm supposed to really see here?"

Becoming a Determined Person

Author and poet Ella Wheeler Wilcox said: "There is no chance, no destiny, no fate that can circumvent or hinder or control the firm resolve of a determined person or a determined soul." Here are three ways to become a determined person.

1. *Keep Your Eyes on the Prize.* The moment you take your eyes off the prize, goal, or finish line, that's the moment you will start having problems. What you focus on, you

will gravitate to. What you don't look at will begin to distance itself away from you. What you respect comes to you, but what you disrespect runs from you.

2. *Look for the Opportunities in the Struggle.* When you transition your mind to be determined and have a strong will, every situation becomes an opportunity for another door to be open to your life. This is because determined people find bad situations as good opportunities, and they dig for the lessons. I remember being in a situation where there was a misunderstanding where I could have gotten upset, frustrated, or disrespectful. But instead, I saw it as an opportunity to be the bigger person, even while I endured disrespect and shame. My determination led me to smile, even when I knew people didn't appreciate me, and it helped me to do my job effectively when I had no one in my corner. It has since given me more stamina and strength to endure when in other tough situations. I'm actually grateful for the bad way I was treated, because it made me a better person.

3. *Forgive Others and Yourself.* If you remain unforgiving, it will chain you to the bitterness of your past. If you can't forgive, then you won't last, and you certainly won't gain. Forgiveness is such a powerful act that you almost can't be in the power of Now without it.

Life is Like a Toll Road

The mistake we often make is to think that when we are going through good times, life is good. I'm not saying that's not a fact, but in some cases it's not. For instance, you could be having a superb vacation, but at the same time you are racking up a huge bill, or you could be having a great party, but find out later that it was a bad idea, because it took energy away from work the next day.

WISDOM KEY

THE THINGS
YOU REFUSE
TO <u>CONFRONT</u>
WILL SOMEDAY
<u>CONQUER</u> YOU

One of the lessons my dad passed down to me, which I often share is that "Life is like a toll road. You will either pay when you get on or you are going to pay when you're getting off." The idea is to pay your dues while you have the strength and energy to gain the resources you need to remit those payments. That way, when you get off you owe nothing.

Nobody thinks of the benefits of their process when they are getting up early in the mornings going to work day after day, having to journey through bad weather, and dealing with difficult bosses and co-workers. Nobody sees the promotions that are on the way because of hard work, stress, and tiredness—the process that causes him or her to move up in the company and learn so many lessons that could help them to open their own businesses. But the reality is that it is doing just that.

Three Strategies to Living Through It

There are many strategies to help you live through challenges in your life. I have covered several already in this chapter. Three other pragmatic ideas include: living in a positive environment, surrounding yourself with voices of truth, and embracing yourself.

First, find a positive environment that you use as your safe haven. Your positive environment may come in different forms. For example, it could be a coffee house, a library, the beach, or a park bench in a quiet park. One of those places for me is my mother's home. I've traveled around the world, and I have stayed in some of the best five-star hotels and resorts money can buy, but when it comes to that familiar tranquil habitat, my mother's house is the place for me to go.

We all need to have that safe environment that we can go to when we are having tough times, whether it's in the home of an old mentor, your grandparents, or your childhood church. It's the place where you are drawn to, not because of the hype energy of events, but because of the peace and freedom that allow you to cry freely, to speak openly, or to pray quietly or loudly. It's that safe environment that allows you to be yourself, where you are free from performing.

Second, you need to surround yourself with people who will speak the truth. We call them truth tellers. Truth doesn't mean correction or instructions; it means revealing the vulnerability of what's really happening in your life and the possibilities of what can happen.

People who speak the truth don't just say what's wrong; they also say how things can be right. That's how you know someone is a truth teller. Someone who's criticizing is just giving the facts of the situation or being a fact teller. For example, they'll tell you that you look overweight or under-dressed, and that may be a fact. But that doesn't mean that you can't lose the weight or dress better. So, it is important to have a voice of truth that's speaking in your life. Whatever you do, find some truth in the midst of what's going on, and let that be a compass for you.

Third, embrace yourself. There were seasons in my life when I felt extremely inadequate as a singer and actor. There will always be those moments of insecurity where the bigger the opportunity or the more significant the thing is that you are about to go through, the less competent you may feel. I had to embrace myself. That means you have to be okay with the fact that you are not as good as you think, or that you are better than you think you are. You have to embrace all of it—the good, the bad and the ugly.

The reason I think this is important is because we tend to play the blame game, and at the same time disqualify ourselves as we face those difficult moments. Here are some of the thoughts we may entertain as we go through those tough times: *"I don't qualify for this. I can't make it through this. I'm not strong enough for this part. There's a mistake somewhere; this shouldn't have been me.*

It should have been better than this. It should have been somebody else. What have I done to deserve this?"

Whether it was by chance, circumstances, or purpose, you are where you find yourself now. Therefore, you have to embrace you because the only person who really feels the core of your struggles is you. If you don't have that needed self-motivation to help you, it doesn't matter what song or words of encouragement you get. It won't have the impact if you don't first recognize that you can believe in you when no one else does.

Don't Scarf Down the Meal of Life

As you are reading this book right now, you are going through something. It might be minor issues with your body or transitional issues with your kids moving from one school to the next. It's almost like eating a meal. If you eat it too fast, you might end up sick because your body can only digest so much at one time. So, you have to cut it up, chew it properly, taste all the flavors, drink some water to wash it down, and wait until it is completely digested.

So it is with life. When you're going through things, some meat can be tougher than others, and some dishes taste better than others. I know with the bad dishes you just want to scarf it down, but you have to take your time and eat it. And just like life, a lot of stuff that doesn't taste the best is usually the best for you, and those that taste the sweetest are usually the worst things for you.

What makes it easier not to scarf down the meal of life is seasoning it with purpose. In the next chapter, I will focus on how to discover purpose as you live The Now Way of Life.

In Summary

How we live through a difficult season in our lives is a choice. We can decide to quit. We can decide to act without purpose. We can decide to do it alone or ask for help. We can get so focused on asking why things happened that we don't see how we can move on and learn from it. Moving through situations is a process and it requires perseverance.

Practice

1. *Take out a piece of paper and make a list of the five most challenging seasons you have had to live through. For example, one of my challenging seasons was at age 17 when I found out that I was going to be a father.*

_____

_____

_____

_____

_____

2. *Next to each challenge, write down the strategies you used to live through it back then.*

_____

_____

_____

_____

_____

_____

_____

_____

_____

_____

_____

_____

_____

_____

3. *Now, based on what you have read so far, what different strategies would you employ if a similar situation arose?*

_____

_____

_____

_____

_____

_____

_____

_____

_____

_____

_____

_____

_____

"With every experience and with every encounter, I live in the NOW, and it has changed my life."

JAVEN

On the TV set hosting Kathy LEE Gifford and Nicole C. Mullen.

On the set of my TV Show "Now Living" in London, England.

On set hosting a music special in Los Angeles, CA.

Backstage with NFL Hall of Famer Dan Marino after a big show.

*Backstage with motivational speaker Les Brown
on the Get Motivated Tour.*

*On location hosting with the President of TBN,
Matt & his wife, Laurie Crouch.*

My son's graduation from UCF, a proud dad.

Great show with legendary news anchorman Dan Rather.

At work with our Annual Summer Slam Sport Camp that we offer to over 200 underprivileged youth every year!

*Working behind the scenes with pop star Nick Jonas
for a performance on the AMAs!*

*On set as "Prince Tarshish" with actor Luke Goss
for the movie **One Night with the King**.*

*On location in India for the movie **One Night with the King**
with the great Omar Sharif.*

On set hosting the legendary Clark Sisters.

Behind the scenes with Joel & Victoria Osteen
for a special TV taping.

Performing at the LA DREAM CENTER
one of my favorite places to sing!

Interviewing Brian "Head" Welch from
the heavy metal band "Korn"!

Hitting the red carpet at the Dove Awards.

Interviewing country legend Reba McEntire.

At Capital Records working with pop star
Demi Lovato in the studio.

Grace CD charts at #8 on gospel Billboard opening week!

CHAPTER SEVEN

DISCOVERING PURPOSE

Purpose is a constant discovery of the many layers of life that has the ability to speak to our legacy for the next generation that we are a part of. For many people, discovering real purpose happens too late or never at all. Often we don't want to know our true purpose because of the price that comes with it. So we fill our lives with busy schedules and meaningless goals only to yearn for more.

Yet our purpose existed long before we got here, and it is a part of the connections to our generation, lineage, our children, and our children's children. So, it's not just personal, it's also collective.

Purpose is something you may never really get credit for. You will be rewarded for fulfilling goals, visions, and specific accomplishments, but you will probably never hear applause for purpose. When you are done

> **WISDOM KEY**
>
> You don't <u>DECLARE</u> your purpose; you DISCOVER and <u>ACCEPT</u> it

with your part—in the sense that you take your final breath—the hope is that you would have connected with enough people to pass the baton of purpose on, so they can continue the work. We see this with Martin Luther King Jr. and all the people he's touched with the civil rights movement. We also see this with families who are in businesses, like Sam Walton's family, who has continued the purpose and legacy of Walmart, making merchandise available to Americans in a very affordable way.

Living out your purpose is more of a discovery than declaring what it is. You don't declare your purpose; you discover and you accept it. It's really something you receive and are a part of. When you do that, it begins to open you up to greater and bigger things that will long outlive what you've been called to do.

Your Vision and Future

Vision is crucial to purpose. It's important to cultivate what it means to have a real vision for your life because it connects you to your purpose. Without it, we are not able to see the value of life.

When I use the word "vision," I'm not referring to what you see with your eyes, but what you see with your mind, for example, an insight, or mental view of your children's future, your career, business, or your personal life. This is about how you see yourself, not only today but also years down the road. What is your vision telling you? How are you cultivating that vision?

Real vision involves planning. If it doesn't have the planning element, it's really not a vision. It's an illusion. It's daydreaming.

A real vision has a plan where you are able to see how you can get from point A to point B and take it all the way home.

Seeing your future is one of the hardest things you will have to do in life, yet it's one of the most profitable habits you can develop if you are disciplined enough to do so. Most people just wish and hope for the best, but it's crucial to ask what future you imagine for yourself.

Facts can be very loud, but even louder should be your faith because what you believe will determine what you will receive. I always say, "*Pay attention to your faith,*" because it will tell you what your outcome will be, what your new present is going to look like, and what your Now is going to produce.

Prayer and Purpose

One of the most powerful ways to discover and accept your purpose is through prayer. Prayer is a conversation with God. It's not a wish list. It's not a ritual of any kind. It's really just having a conversation that speaks from the heart or speaks from the spirit of who you are.

We're made up of three entities—body, soul, and spirit, Psychologists talk about the spiritual vacuum or void that we all have, the part of us that can be filled with something eternal. Unfortunately, we sometimes see famous and rich people commit suicide because they may have never filled that void with something bigger than their career, their money, or their relationships.

How extraordinary it is to communicate with a more supreme being! How amazing it is to express that spiritual life and love! I know many people who are very skeptical about having a dialogue with God. "What if we are talking to nothing?" they would ask. "What if it doesn't work?" But what if we are talking to someone, and what if it does work?

> **WISDOM KEY**
>
> REAL LEADERSHIP CAN BE DEFINED AS THE ACT OF ONE BEGGAR LETTING OTHER BEGGARS KNOW WHERE THE BREAD IS

Prayer works for many people. This is why I encourage others to develop a prayer life. It doesn't matter if it's just two words, a thank you towards the heavens, or a kneeling at your bedside, reflecting on all the good things that happened and asking for help for the challenges you're facing. Prayer may be an extraordinary tool that we push aside or don't use enough, but whatever the situation and however you choose to do it, prayer is effective and can produce good results. So many times I have prayed and watched God give me exactly what I was praying for. I've seen it work in my finances, issues with my health and in my personal goals.

Prayer also gives you the opportunity to listen and the leisure to connect spiritually with a higher power that takes you beyond this natural world. A perfect example is when our spirits dream while we are asleep. You can dream of places you've never been or of experiences you've never had. How do you explain that?

You really can't. Scientists have tried. This is why it's important to allow your faith to believe in the possibilities, the extraordinary and the supernatural, and pray accordingly. Then you will receive what you believe in your heart and spirit.

God is a loving God, and He doesn't require anything but that we love Him back and do our best to become our best selves, through prayer and fulfilling our purpose. That takes faith.

Faith and Purpose

Faith is believing in the impossible. It's not just hoping and wishing; it is coupled with expectancy and then action. Real faith is literally acting out that which you know is going to happen.

It doesn't require great faith to believe in what you can clearly see. Rather, you need simple faith. For example, if there's a chair, you're going to sit on it. You believe the chair is going to hold you when you sit. You don't know the weight capacity of that chair. You don't know if the screws are loose. You don't know if the glue will hold. You don't know if the legs are going to slide out from under you. But you believe that whoever made this chair has done it in a way that will hold you up.

So it is with life. There are many things that we can believe instead of being a pessimist, saying things like, "I don't believe; it's not going to happen." Instead, we should challenge ourselves to act on the possibility that we will be a part of a great purpose and destiny. I believe, therefore, I am, and because I am, I will do.

Whatever it is that you're doing—whether you know it or not—that's what you believe. So, don't tell me you have faith in your marriage if all your actions toward your spouse are negative. What are you doing to express your confident expectations in your union with your spouse? Are you taking time for date nights? Are you compromising? Are you keeping peace in the home? If not, chances are you don't really have faith in your marriage.

Practically expressing faith is also applicable to other areas of your life, like your career. If you believe that you are going to be the leader of the company, yet you always come to work late, gripe about extra duties, and complain about your salary, here again your actions contradict your belief.

Faith plays a major role in the foundation of life. Believe it or not, we all have a measure of it. We all believe in something. It could be our little pets or the ability to do whatever it is that we do. We don't think twice about the things that we believe in: we just act on them with faith, believing that they will produce the results that we need them to.

Let's look at the example of a guitar player. He believes in his musicianship, and therefore he steps out, takes that guitar, and begins to act out what it means to play. If I don't believe that I can play, clearly, I'm not going to try, and I'm certainly not going to take lessons and put forth the effort.

We all have some level of faith in what we do. Some people believe in the economic system; some believe in the political system. Others believe in love, and the list goes on. Whatever we believe in becomes a very strong force that allows us to push past our inabilities.

Our faith also pushes us past our boundaries. When we can't go any further, our faith takes us on. Faith keeps you going. It keeps you striving. It keeps you pressing and pushing and reaching toward the things that are just beyond you. I couldn't write this book for you if I didn't have the faith that I could get it done and that I really have something important for you to read.

Our faith is extraordinary and, in some ways, magical. It can really do supernatural things for us if we tap into it the right way and for the right reasons. If you have faith in love, it's going to be a huge part of your life because you are going to act and respond to all things with love. Even when somebody else sees it in a different way, you're going to see it through the eyes of love because of your faith.

WISDOM KEY

YOU CAN'T EXPECT PEOPLE TO <u>SEE</u> IN YOU WHAT YOU DON'T SEE IN <u>YOURSELF</u>

Faith also requires us to be persistent. This means when you have real faith, you don't just throw it away by quitting. It is a fight that is beyond your fight. It is a tenacity that is beyond your tenacity. It's a pattern, not a one-time thing.

Hoping and wishing for something is a one-time thing, but faith, on the other hand, is a journey that says, "I know this is going to come to pass so I'm sticking with it; I position and prepare myself. I'm readying myself for this outcome because I know it's going to be exactly the way I see it in my mind's eye, the way I see it in my spirit, the way I see it in how I perceive things to be."

Faith pushes you to stay steady and consistent. It's the difference between someone running a sprint race and a marathon. Yes, there are times when instant manifestations will occur when faith is activated; however, there will be times when faith will have you continuously pushing and pressing forth relentlessly. Some journeys demand speed, while others require patience and endurance.

Real faith is powerful. It almost takes the place of reality; it can literally structure or restructure one's entire life. Faith positions you to act in the way and direction that you believe in. In that way, faith is very positive. In that same way, if you put your faith in things that are carnal, temporary, negative, and harmful, it can be just as dangerous as it is positive. It's a very strong force.

That's why I encourage people to put their faith in eternal things. Put your faith in things that are going to last, things that are going to be positive for you and for the people around you, things that are going to be a part of a legacy, and things that contribute to purpose. It's okay to have faith in the economic system, but you better have faith that goes beyond because we all know that the economy can fail us. It's okay to believe in our political system, but you've got to have faith beyond that because we know that the political system has failed us and will fail us in many ways. When this happens, our faith will propel us forward. It will give us the strength and energy we need to go on, in spite of how we feel.

We tap into our faith with what information we are taking in, what words are being taught to us, and what is being prayed for us. We tap into it by acting it out—taking faith steps. If the only thing that you are living on is practicality, life for you is going to be extremely limited with a void of greatness and true success.

It takes faith to truly live. It takes believing to see things that are not there. In your spirit, you'll see and hear them. In your spirit, you can even feel them and know that it is going to come to pass. You're not wishing, you're not hoping. You just know. When you have that level of faith, there's nothing that you cannot do.

Faith and Possibilities

In a moment, I'm going to talk to you about staying open to possibilities, which can lead you to discovering your purpose. To stay open to possibilities and discover your purpose, you need faith. This we can find in different ways. For some of us, it's through supportive friends and family. For others, it's through religion and belief in God. Still others turn to their creative community for nourishment.

At the end of the day, when you are lying in bed, sleepless at 3 a.m., or trying something you never had before, faith is what will get you through. Outside forces can encourage and strengthen you, but faith has to be chosen from within. By now you should know that music is in my soul, but it also helps me to embrace the possibilities in every Now Season. Before we turn to the next chapter, I'd like to share with you a song I wrote about faith. Many years ago, keeping the faith got me through a very tough season in my life and it became the title song of my album.

⤞⤝

Keeping the Faith

Sometimes it gets hard I don't know where to start, I feel all alone
Keep pushing and trying through test and trials, I gotta be strong,
I don't know if I can have the dreams I've seen,
but I know that it will happen if I just believe.
So, I'm hoping and praying, believing things will change

Oh oh keeping the faith
Oh oh I gotta keep the faith
Oh oh keeping the faith
Oh oh I gotta keep the faith

See I know you've been down for quite some time and it seems
like there's nothing that will ease your mind
But you've gotta be strong even though you don't know
Just how things will end
But in time things will work out for your good
Hold on and pray just like you should

'Cause things will be fine, it just takes time
But you'll be alright

Oh oh keeping the faith
Oh oh I gotta keep the faith
Oh oh keeping the faith
Oh oh I gotta keep the faith

You're going to look for me and I'll be a long time gone
Hanging out with my friends talk about how it all went down
How He changed my life complete and how He turned it
all around
Oh oh keeping the faith
Oh oh I gotta keep the faith
Oh oh keeping the faith
Oh oh I gotta keep the faith

∽

In Summary

Purpose is different from goals, vision, or objectives. Purpose lives within each of us and is your God-given legacy to yourself, your family, and the world around you. Discovering your purpose is essential to living in the Now; otherwise, you will drift through the seasons of your life without fulfillment. One of the most powerful ways to discover purpose is through prayer. Prayer is conversation with God, who is greater than you. Believing in God and prayer are exercises of faith. One of the aspects of our humanity is that we are able to walk through life without despair.

∽

Practice

1. *Answer these questions about your purpose.*

    • *What do you believe is your purpose?*

    _____

    _____

    _____

    _____

    _____

    _____

    _____

    _____

    _____

    _____

- *Have you discovered your purpose through prayer?*

- *What do you think is holding you back from living a purposeful life?*

_____

_____

_____

_____

_____

_____

_____

_____

_____

_____

_____

_____

_____

CHAPTER EIGHT

STAYING OPEN TO POSSIBILITIES

Many people don't understand what the word possibility means. When they say something is possible, they often are saying that a thing has the potential to do something, make something happen, or achieve the full capacity of its purpose. I think these definitions are too limiting.

Instead, the way you stay open to possibilities is to remember the expression: "The sky is not the limit. You can go beyond the sky." Your legacy has the potential to live far beyond the reach of the stars. When you impact somebody's life, change someone's circumstance, give hope to a hopeless situation or hug someone who needs it at a crucial time, you change the trajectory of his or her life.

Ask yourself the question, "What do I want my legacy to be?" and know that that's endless. Know that you achieve your legacy by filling every crevice, corner, inch and entity with extraordinary things, whatever they may be. Extraordinary doesn't have to be flashy, but it does need to be filled with your life. Staying open to possibilities is having the willingness to dream and explore again.

Control Can be an Illusion

When you remain open to the things that are possible, you are exercising the willingness to release control. Control can be an illusion. Just when you think you're in control, you're not. And in reality, you never really are in control of the narrative, situation, and circumstances. Believing you are in control prevents you from really understanding how important it is to embrace all of what can be, what should be, or what will be as you go along in this journey of life.

You stay open by not putting the lid on. When you're in control, everything is limited to your capacity—your stress level, your physical reach, or your financial situation.

Here's a powerful story about control. A man was angry with his young daughter for wasting money when she decorated a box with expensive gold wrapping paper. He was even angrier when she gave it to him, and he discovered it was empty. He yelled at her, "When you give someone a present, there is supposed to be something inside!"

With tears in her eyes, she said, "Oh, Daddy, it's not empty at all. I blew kisses into the box. They're all for you." The father was crushed and begged for her forgiveness. A short time later, an accident took the life of the little girl. Whenever the father became discouraged with life, he would take an imaginary kiss out of that gold box and remember the love of the child who had put it there.

The father, who wanted to be in control at that moment, exemplified those of us who limit our future based on our present. The father would never have had the gift of kisses from his daughter if he had stifled her with his control. Living in the Now says that we are building something extraordinary that leaves the door open for something even more extraordinary.

Think of it this way. Do you think that "almost" is a good word?' Nobody wants to almost get paid back. You don't want to almost die, and you don't want somebody to almost love you. No what you want is the absolute most.

Hope for the Best

Hoping for the best and staying open to possibilities go hand in hand. You can't hope without being open. Openness positions your heart to receive the best of what you hope for. When you're open to the possibilities in life, it is only then that you can receive what you hope for. It is also then that you will come into the greatest version of the outcome for any situation.

That's what I had to do as a 17-year-old boy. I went from being young and free to becoming a father burdened with responsibilities. But in spite of these unexpected responsibilities, I needed to understand that the possibilities were still endless, and this could be extraordinary. I needed to position myself for a great future and finish college. I also needed to see myself as being a great light and parent to this little bundle of joy. I needed to hope—to actually know—that I would make it.

IN LIFE, YOU DON'T GET WHAT YOU DESERVE, YOU GET WHAT YOU CAN NEGOTIATE

In previous chapters, I talked about how you need to be careful about the atmosphere you live in. That's absolutely vital in staying open to possibilities. If as a young father I had surrounded myself with people who were negative, my journey would have been much harder.

You can't put yourself in a pessimistic environment and expect to stay optimistic. I'd love to say friends don't matter, but friends play a role in a big way. And what we are listening to matters, too. A song can shift your whole attitude about life. The right song at the right time can change everything, just like the wrong song at the wrong time can change everything. The words you're hearing are crucial to how you stay open to possibilities.

I think of Eminem's song, "Lose Yourself." It's almost like a war cry, especially because of his upbringing—coming up in poverty and not knowing if he would make it. Considered one of the best hip-hop songs of all time, the song became the first hip-hop music number to win an Academy Award, and by 2017 had more than 10 million downloads in the United States alone. It has become an inspirational song to countless people across the world, simply because of the effectiveness of the lyrics:

Look, if you had one shot, or one opportunity
To seize everything you ever wanted, in one moment,
Would you capture it or just let it slip?
You better lose yourself in the music.
The moment, you own it, you better never let it go.
You only get one shot, do not miss your chance to blow.
This opportunity comes once in a lifetime, yo.
You better lose yourself in the music
The moment, you own it, you better never let it go.
You only get one shot, do not miss your chance to blow.
This opportunity comes once in a lifetime.

Lose Yourself *by EMINEM. Writer/s: JEFFREY IRWIN BASS, LUIS EDGARDO RESTO, MARSHALL B MATHERS Publisher: Kobalt Music Publishing Ltd.*

What music are you listening to? What route do you take to work? What neighborhood did you choose to live in? These are all important questions. Think of it like eating at home or out in a restaurant. Eating out is not just about eating food; it's about having a unique experience in a nice ambience that helps to make you feel good while eating.

Yes, some things are beyond your control, but there are ways to change the environment and the atmosphere without it being costly. Sometimes it's just about taking a different route or switching the mundane routine around. It brings about new possibilities and fresh opportunities.

Here's another piece of advice to up your hope factor—never underestimate what a good conference or seminar can do. There are conferences and seminars for just about every season and for every circumstance and situation in life. There are conferences just for women and conferences just for men, for businesses and entrepreneurships, for leaders, farmers, hair stylists, and politicians—for just about every profession or industry under the sun. These events can be empowering and could therefore recharge your subconscious and make you want to hit the ground running when you return home.

So what are your hopes? What do you believe is possible in your life? When you study the origin of the word "hope," you will find that it comes from the Old English "hopian," meaning to wish, expect, or look forward to. So, when we hope, we are saying: it's possible to find the right person to share our lives with; it's possible to find the right job, one that will pay a good salary; and it's possible to have the career I dream about. That's what hope is.

When you have hope, it means that you have possibilities, not just wishes and fantasies. The reality is there is no absolute guarantee in life, there's no certainty that if you got the right degree that you're going to get the right job, or that if you are a nice, kind, and loving person, that you're going to meet the kind and loving person that is perfect for you.

But you can flip that same statement and ask the question, "Is it possible to meet that kind of a person, attain a good job, or have a satisfying career?" Well, the answer would be, "absolutely yes!"

The Power of Imagination

Albert Einstein once said: "Imagination is more important than knowledge. For knowledge is limited to all we now know and understand, while imagination embraces the entire world, and all there ever will be to know and understand."

Imagination is its own form of courage. It is so powerful that it makes it possible to experience a whole world inside of the mind. It gives the ability to look at any situation from a different point of view and to mentally explore the past and the present while developing the future.

Imagination is not limited only to seeing pictures in your mind. It also includes all the five senses and your emotions. You can imagine a sound, taste, smell, physical sensation, or emotion. For some people, it is effortless to see mental pictures. Others find it easier to imagine a feeling, and still others are more comfortable imagining the sensation of one of the five senses. When you begin to train your imagination, it gives the ability to combine all of these senses to create an incredible outcome.

A developed and strong imagination does not make you a daydreamer or impractical. It's quite the opposite; it strengthens your creative abilities and is a great tool for re-creating and remodeling your world and life. This starts the path of taking actions that will catapult your Now into an endless future of possibilities.

Let's use your imagination in this scenario. What if you were to receive a phone call from your local senator's office informing you that you are one of four citizens the president might visit in their home? What would you do? Would you turn down the invitation and make excuses of why you or your home are not ready for such a visit? Would you live the next several months with doubts that someone like you could ever be selected for this opportunity?

Or would you begin to prepare for the possibility of such a high honor? Would you allow yourself to be stirred up with the hope that you and your family were about to have the experience of a lifetime in your own home with the most powerful man in this free world?

My hope is that you would do the latter—that you would begin to prepare for the "possibility" of a presidential visit. And if you believe that the president of the United States might actually show up for dinner at your house, you would begin to do all that you could do to prepare your household by obtaining the best food and making your home look its best.

The idea here is that you are preparing for something great—not because you know for certain it will happen, but because there is a strong "possibility" that it will. And because there is this possibility, you prepare for a hopeful outcome.

The Power of Preparation

So many people take action without preparation and end up not being ready for possibilities. To prepare means to plan, but in order to do so, you will have to take into consideration these key questions: *What is the expected outcome or purpose? What is it that I am looking to accomplish?*

For example, if you knew Calvin Klein or Mark Jacobs might want to use you as a model to walk the runway—even though you have no experience as a professional model—you wouldn't just sit around and not try to get yourself prepared. Although you may not be as tall or thin as the average model, you would still attempt to prepare yourself so that you can be the best version of you when you walk down that runway.

Here's what we tend to forget—there are innumerable possibilities awaiting our attention. So often, however, we aren't ready to pursue them. I remember getting involved in a drama class in college. For my final exam, I did Sidney Poitier's character "Walter" from the classic 1961 film, *A Raisin in the Sun*. At this time in my life, I was wrapping up my degree in psychology while travelling every weekend as a professional singer in a band. I was also part of one of the popular fraternities at the college and a big brother to one of the popular girls' sororities.

I didn't have enough time to prepare, but I did my best and received a standing ovation. For me, acting was something that came naturally, but it was not on my radar. I was just taking the class as an elective because I kind of liked it, and it was an opportunity for me to fulfill the credits needed to complete my degree.

This didn't stop my drama professor from approaching me about taking acting more seriously. "You really should hone in on this, Javen," he encouraged. "You have something there, and you could do this!"

But I dismissed his advice, thinking, "Pastors' kids don't become actors. People from Hollywood, Florida, don't make it in Hollywood, California. Black men don't become stars."

In my mind, acting meant being a star. I didn't understand that although acting is an incredible craft and career, it doesn't necessarily involve fame or fortune. There are many great actors who are not stars yet have fulfilled their purpose in life while having a satisfying, successful, and financially rewarding career.

Many years later, having done several feature films, commercials, and off-Broadway productions, I realize how wrong I was in not preparing. I often wonder how much further I could have gone in my acting career had I better prepared for opportunities in film and theater. How many more auditions could I have nailed if I worked on my craft back then? I am challenging you to prepare for your future. That nudge from a professor, inspired word from a pastor, push from a coach or talk from your mentor could be a sign of what is to come. Believe it or not, something big is about to happen in your life, but will you be prepared when it does?

Avoiding Distractions

Let me continue the story of this time in college with a discussion about distractions. I was sidetracked by what I thought was important during those years. For me, the drama team was not the "it" team to be a part of. They weren't the popular kids everybody wanted to be around. Instead, they were a somewhat isolated group on campus and the "weird" ones in some ways.

But if you were able to hit a note, grab a microphone, and woo a crowd in song, then you were a member of the popular groups. And that's what I wanted to be—one of the popular kids. Therefore, I pushed drama to the side.

Many of us do that in life. We have opportunities that are immediately in front of us, yet we overlook them because we attach more value to our distractions. Or we are hoping for a quick fix and an easy way out, which only leads us to places of compromise where we settle for less than we are worth.

For example, think about a relationship you settled for that ended up in ruins. If you knew there was a better relationship in your future, you might not have wasted time being treated the way you were treated.

WISDOM KEY

YOU CAN ALWAYS TELL HOW FAR A PERSON WILL GO IN THEIR FUTURE BY THE SET OF FRIENDS THEY WILL HANG OUT WITH

The same thing happens with our children and how we handle them—allowing them to sit around and waste precious time on video games and cell phones while brushing aside more meaningful and productive activities and opportunities. In truth, as parents we can be clueless to the type of children we are raising.

If you are a parent reading this book, you should know that you might be raising the next president of the United States or the next CEO of a major Fortune 500 company. Some of these distractions may not be negative—they are just good things that consume more time and energy than needed.

In Summary

Possibilities are aligned with your purpose and legacy. There are many ways to open yourself up to possibilities and then walk through the door. Letting go of control and embracing hope clear the way for possibilities. Then letting the powers of imagination and preparation take over will move you forward. At the same time, be careful of distractions, which can take you off the road to possibilities.

Practice

1. *Name three impossibilities in your past that became possible. (Trust me, we all have them.)*

_____

_____

_____

_____

_____

2. *List three impossibilities you are facing now, and give one example of how each impossibility can become possible.*

_____

_____

_____

_____

_____

_____

3. *Answer the question, "How did I overcome impossibilities, and what helped me?"*

_____

_____

_____

_____

_____

_____

4. *As you begin to reflect and recall, start applying the information you derived from your answer to current situations that seem impossible.*

CHAPTER NINE

OVERCOMING OBSTACLES IN YOUR NOW SEASON

A man watched a butterfly for several hours as it struggled to force its body through a small opening in its cocoon. When the butterfly stopped making progress, he decided to help by snipping off the remaining bit of the cocoon with scissors. The butterfly emerged, but it had a swollen body and small, shriveled wings.

The man waited for the wings to enlarge, but it did not happen. The poor butterfly was unable to fly and eventually died. What the man had failed to understand was that the struggle of the butterfly getting through the small opening was nature's way of forcing fluid from its body into its wings so it could fly.

Without struggles, we never grow and get stronger. And while help from others is wonderful, we need to develop our own strength as we move through life. Strength comes from sticking to something and seeing it through until the end, regardless of the pain. That's why quitting can be a poor strategy if you want more.

For many people, stopping is an option when things get hard because it seems so inviting. The growing process requires going through all parts of what we consider a problem or challenge. If the only thing you experience is the initial problem, then you are shortchanging the process. If you take the challenge and see it all the way, then it becomes a tool you can use to activate the wisdom you gain from it.

Hardwired to Quit?

Stopping is something that is a very natural thing to do. You almost will inevitably try to stop anything that is progressive in your life because if it is to be successful, it will require challenge and discipline. If you're trying to lose weight, when you first start running, your body is not going to necessarily say, "Yea, let's keep running!" Rather, it's going to initially tell you, "Not today!"

The same goes for other paths to progress in life—paths that require discipline, self-motivation, and efforts to push through challenges and struggles. There is always this natural ability to throw in the towel, which becomes much easier to do as we get older in life.

Would you say then that we are hardwired to quit? In my opinion, we are. Not only are we wired to quit, we are also hardwired to find comfort. Our taste buds exemplify this best. If we put something in our mouth that doesn't taste good and comforting, we would more than likely stop eating. Babies and little children are perfect examples of this behavior. They let you know really fast if something tastes bad to them—just duck!

Attitude Determines Altitude

In spite of our innate ability to avoid discomfort, we can consciously choose to hang in there, thrive, and press through the pressure. We sometimes hear of horrendous survival stories where the survivors endure the impossible or do the unthinkable in order to survive.

I remember the story of a 7-year-old girl who climbed out of the remains of a private plane that had crashed in the middle of a desolate area. That plane crash killed her entire family and all who were on board except her. Determined to seek help, this little child trekked barefooted almost three miles through dark, cold, and dangerous wooded area to find someone who could help her.

It may not come easy, but we can make up in our mind that, "I will not quit." This is the attitude we all have to exercise, so that once we start whatever it is that we are getting ready to start—whether it be a new job, relationship, or a semester in school— we will give ourselves the opportunity to complete and stay with it until the end.

In one of my hit songs, I explored this idea of making up your mind not to quit and how prayer, which we talked about in the last few chapters, can keep you going.

I'm Alright

I get upset and sometimes down
Feeling so lost like no one's around
But I pray hard and one thing I've found
He hears my cry and he never lets me down

Oh, oh I, I'm alright
Oh, oh I, I'm alright
Oh, oh I, I'll be alright

So when you are down and can't find your way
So many questions don't know what to say
Just look up to him and say a little prayer
He'll give you peace and your burdens he'll share
Oh, oh I, I'm alright
Oh, oh I, I'm alright
Oh, oh I, I'll be alright

There's a price to pay when you always stand your ground
And everything you face has got to turn around
'Cause there's no other place to go when you're in need I know
He will see you through and if you believe he'll make it alright

When you check out, you lose out because there is always more to gain each step you take along the way. Think of it as in grade school. Stopping at the first level will disqualify you from getting your diploma.

As you continue, each challenge will provide the tools you need for the next level of opportunities. The more challenges you can endure and conquer, the more responsibility you will be able to take on. The more responsibility you can carry will determine the more opportunities you will be prepared to pursue. This is why you cannot afford to quit because it literally determines your future's net worth.

I often think about the repercussion of a person only having an elementary-school education. That person's life will go on, and he or she will get older; however, their mind-set and education level will be very limited.

So it is with life. Sometimes we are faced with the toughest challenges, and instead of going through them, we stop somewhere in the middle. Hence, we give up our own rights to process the things that are designed to equip us with more knowledge, wisdom, and understanding.

We cannot see all the resources and benefits of what's going to happen once we complete this particular season in our lives. However, choosing to press through your process means that you've accepted the opportunity to gain the benefits. If you can learn to endure what you're in now, the stuff that's to come will be easier because life gets more manageable as you press forward and learn how to solve, resolve, and walk through challenging situations.

Moving can either mean that you are in a recurring cycle of a particular situation or that you are projecting forward, where you are persevering and growing from the different obstacles you face. So to gain is not just about movement alone, but rather, it's about forward projection.

You can learn from people who did not stop or quit on their relationships. When they have their birthdays, anniversaries, or special celebratory moments in their lives, you can't find a seat to put their friends and loved ones in. There are so many people who care about them and want to celebrate them because they didn't quit on those people.

Think Challenges, Not Problems

We won't win if we look at our struggles as problems: a problem child, a problem job, a problem marriage, and a problem body. When we do, it means that we've already concluded that it is a negative thing with a negative ending, and this is not healthy for our Now. So, let's change the blueprint of our thinking, and identify our issues to be "challenges," not "problems."

The good thing about a challenge is that you have the ability to defeat it and become the champion in the game of life. You may not win every round, but you can still win the fight. When you look at the game of basketball, it goes right down to the final time on the score. You're sometimes talking about two or five seconds down. It doesn't matter how many quarters a team may have lost; they could come back in that last quarter at that very last second and win the championship.

So, what you need to do in your Now Moment is first see all of your problems as challenges in which you are going to be a champion, a winner. You cannot become a winner unless you get into the fight, and nobody gets into a fight unless they think they are going to win. This is why so many people refuse to move forward, because they have a losing mentality.

WISDOM KEY

THE THINGS YOU REFUSE TO CONFRONT WILL SOMEDAY CONQUER YOU

To conquer this, try envisioning yourself as a winner. There's a possibility that you can beat cancer, bring up your grades, get that degree, or get out of debt. You don't have to be among those who choose to drop out; you can get back in the fight of life.

Yes, it's a challenge, and you may feel like you're not ready or can't win the entire fight. But that shouldn't stop you. You can do what any fighter would do—take a break. Take a time-out and rest your legs, get some water, a massage, or go talk to a coach who will help you strategize. Then get back in.

Many of us messed up because we didn't have those life coaches and mentors to point us in the right direction so we could get back in and fight to win. Just because you lost that one round doesn't mean the battle is over. It simply means that you've lost that one round. But there are a few more rounds to go that you need to be prepared for.

Find out what things you need to change. For example, how do you need to re-approach your spouse before you talk to him or her the next time after a disagreement? How do you need to handle your children? How do you spend your money now that you have a better job and resources coming in? Get rejuvenated, get pumped up, and then, in the face of your challenge, declare: "I will come out on top because I am a champion!"

When Perception Becomes Reality

So many people have lived their entire lives carrying loads of unresolved issues that may have stemmed from poor choices, misfortunes, and misconceptions. Whether it's something from our past or the challenge we are currently facing, we tend to want to wish it away, hoping that one day we won't have to deal with it.

But it's important for you to know that you have the keys and tools right in front of you, in your Now Moments, that can help you overcome. If we utilize these very tools, we won't have to wait on that relationship to relinquish our loneliness. We won't have to wait until we are older or have a degree in order to make sound decisions, be courageous, or be bold. We won't have to wait for tomorrow or next year because we can overcome these challenges in our Now.

My life has been a daily process of challenging myself to conquer fears that sent me on a roller coaster of unnecessary and difficult emotions. I would walk away from many encounters and be disturbed about them, even though these thoughts and emotions had nothing to do with the people, meetings, concerts, and shows. However, it had everything to do with me and learning how to dissect information and overcome my fictitious perception of what took place.

There are times when we hear things that were not said and assume something that just wasn't the case. This may come about because of past encounters with people and situations that we have not settled. Consequently, we develop a type of paranoia or a constant warring psychologically or mentally. Our perceptions of people and things become blurred as we use our issues with one person to judge the other person, or we take one situation and use it as the premise for other situations that didn't deserve that type of pre-judgment.

Things begin to worsen because we refuse to handle the matter at hand or deal with the real core of the issue we are experiencing. We drag things out and become immune to our now developed insecurity, which only stemmed from a past unrelated challenge. Over time, this has trained our thinking process and controls how we act and speak in innocent affairs.

When this happens, we begin to create an atmosphere of suspicion, negativity, or both. Sometimes the attitude will shift toward aggressiveness or an unwillingness to participate with current activities. This goes on for a while, and eventually the people around us begin to respond to what we are putting out. Even a dog can tell when a person doesn't want him around or when the attitude is so intense that it's best he is not around.

When this begins to take place in a person's mind and attitude, their perception has just graduated to reality. Because everything in that person's atmosphere will begin to feed off of the perception that's being portrayed. My question to you today is what false perception have you created in your life and are you willing to identify it and change it?

You Can't Fall from the Bottom

There was a time in my life when I lost it all—the job, the relationships, and the friends. I remember feeling so low, but it was at my lowest that I began to try everything my heart ever imagined. I reached a point where I just didn't care about any fear of failure anymore, "just do whatever you can imagine" was my thinking. Because of this experience, I believe that it's at your lowest points that you should take your biggest risks. Had you not had one door closed, you would have never discovered the other one. Had you not lost one relationship; you would have never met the awesome person you are with now.

We often hear people say that they were pushed in another direction because of some catastrophic situation like getting laid off. Many entrepreneurs are born as a result of what we think is unfavorable dilemmas. Because of job terminations and people not being able to get rehired, the pressure of linking inner passions to sought-after opportunities has finally caught up and has paved the way for a potentially better future.

This pill may be hard to swallow, but not all the bad experiences you've had up to this point worked against you. They were merely tools to launch you to the next level and give you a better outcome.

We have to remember that life is a journey and that on this journey we are given keys to unlock doors that will lead us to a place of fulfillment. Every situation you encounter gives you a key to unlock a door, to discover something you didn't know was in you or to take you to a higher degree.

Separate the Dark Color Clothes from the White Clothes

Departmentalizing is a key component to overcoming difficult times, because you can only take on and deal with so much at a time. If you don't place your challenges and issues in their respective departments, then you will feel overwhelmed and even begin to believe that your life is one big mistake.

Instead of overcoming, you will feel weighed down, confused, or frustrated, which only causes you to want to quit. This is how people may sometimes fall into serious depression and even go into suicidal thought patterns. It seems like their whole life is worthless, when really, at the heart of the matter, it's a simple issue with a temporary problem that can be resolved. But because they have placed everything into one pile, it becomes too much.

There have been many suicide stories of investors who lost some major financial deals and ran out of money. Consequently, such a person loses sight of what really matters in life. He's so disgruntled that he wants to take his own life, forgetting that he has a beautiful wife, awesome kids, and friends and family who love and care about him. He may not have the money that he once had; however, he's rich in so many other areas of his life.

We see it with people who are in unhealthy relationships. For example, the guy can't let the girl go after she says she doesn't love him anymore, so he kills her and then kills himself. He placed his entire significance in that relationship, failing to realize there is more to life. I like to say it this way: "A broken heart won't kill you unless you let it."

When I talk about departmentalizing all things, I liken it to doing laundry. Taking care of the laundry is not a chore that everyone likes. In fact, it's a hated chore for most people. I'm one of them. I never care to do my own laundry because I actually value my clothes and am always aware of the fact that I don't have the patience or knowledge to properly clean them without destroying them. Let's face it, any good laundry person knows that in order to be effective in keeping your whites white and your colors clear of bleeding out on each other, you need to separate the whites, light color, and dark color clothes. The point is that there has to be serious separation in order for there to be a really successful outcome.

It would be foolish to expect to wash a pile of laundry successfully without first separating them and then washing each

> WISDOM KEY
>
> PEOPLE EVERY-WHERE THINK THEIR WAY IS THE RIGHT WAY

load one at a time. So it is in life. The rebellious child, trust issues with the spouse, the nagging boss, or financial difficulties are all things that have to be kept in their proper space. If we don't separate all these different issues, then we will start imposing things on people and areas in life that don't deserve the judgment or ridicule. We will take matters from home and thrust them on co-workers, and at the same time, take problems from work and charge them to our spouse and family members.

We'll even lay concerns about our children on our best friends, maybe because their children are doing much better than ours. People have suffered the loss of great connections and friendships because of this. Most people have been through enough by the time they meet you, so don't add to their drama.

Departmentalizing the fabrics of your life's affairs isn't as easy as separating whites from colored clothes. But it is systematic and can be done with practice. Here is the two-step process:

1. *Identify and acknowledge the problem.* If you had an unresolved argument with your spouse, it may make you grouchy at work. Consequently, you could get reprimanded for snapping at co-worker. To avoid this, before going too far into your day, ask yourself: "Why am I feeling this way?" Recognize and acknowledge the existence of the problem. If you can't acknowledge the problem, you can't fix the problem, and you have a much bigger problem than the problem itself.

2. *Separate it.* Separating your issues is not an act of being in denial or an excuse to neglect your situation. Rather, it is a responsibility that one takes on to maintain order so one thing doesn't bleed over into the next. It is in separating that you can now give time to evaluate and implement a plan. That way, when you revisit the area, you will hopefully come up with solutions and not more problems.

Little Problems Matter

The old sayings go, "Little hinges swing big doors," and "The devil is in the details." I think both these statements are true. We think that little problems don't matter. I think we are all guilty of this. I know I am. The little nudge in our gut feeling we get about situations. The little thought that says "it's time to walk away" or "it's time to calm down." So many times we are given little warnings in our Now Moments that we refuse to obey, only to face major setbacks.

I was counseling a married couple once and used the analogy of how you can't just run all the red lights and not expect to get a violation. Well, the couple I was counseling stated that they did see all the red lights but kept going. Now, here they sat with major relationship problems and on the verge of divorce. It was all because of all the little red lights that they ignored and kept running through, thinking that they would get to their destination without great penalties.

One of our biggest challenges in life is changing our thinking when it comes to the trivial challenges. Little challenges do matter and they matter greatly, and so be willing to deal with the small, insignificant, seemingly no-big-deal issues as they arise. And when you do, this will help you avoid the possibility of having to deal with an overwhelming mess of a situation in your life later.

Do Some Spring Cleaning

When it comes down to the issues and challenges we face in life, we have to do spring cleaning. I know that for many people, like me, the idea of being that tedious or responsible is asking a lot. I can almost hear your frustration as you're reading this book right now, thinking, "Hey, Javen, you're asking too much. I'd rather let this little thing slide by and just keep it moving."

WISDOM KEY

DON'T LET THE CHALLENGES BECOME YOUR STRUGGLES

Truthfully, not every issue is a big issue, and that is good to know because some challenges we face are extremely simple. But we have to be careful not to make them into bigger issues. This means we shouldn't drag something out that we could have resolved right away because this can create spaces for negativity that may have no merit.

Sometimes it's best to just address the issue by simply asking, "Is this what you meant when you said this?" Or, "I saw a certain thing go this way; can you please explain to me why you did that?" I think simple dialogues like these can resolve most petty things that could potentially become bigger problems. When you have time to brew over something, it can really grow into something bigger and unnecessary.

Negative Trees and Safety Deposit Boxes

Some people will spend years in anguish and defeat and feel sorry for themselves. Things become way bigger than they ever should have been, and the main reason was because they did not allow it to remain small.

Look at it this way. It's like a seed that's planted and watered. If the seed is negativity and gets watered with idle time and other acts of hostility, that seed will begin to take root and grow. And if it continues to grow, it becomes a big and strong tree that's hard to pluck up.

It's a lot easier to dig up a little seed and throw it in the trash as opposed to trying to remove a huge trunk. This is why we need to make sure that we deal with issues while they are in their seed form, or little sprouts, before they become big tree trunks with roots that have taken hold deeply in the soil.

Safety deposit boxes and savings accounts were made to safely keep and store things that add value to our lives, things that we treasure and respect. However, people seem to be locking away hostility and building up issues that are detrimental—things that cause depreciation in their lives.

For example, if I don't learn to overcome hearing someone saying something bad about me today and brushing it off, then I'm going to have a life with a safety deposit box filled with he-said she-said about me, which will affect me for as long as I hold on to it. It's almost like we are taking every negative experience to open savings accounts with, so that we can store up and become wealthy with matters of contention.

When you stop and address these issues, you are emptying out misfortunes from the safety deposit boxes and the saving accounts of your heart. It is only then that your life will be on its way to becoming an overall process of winning and being an overcomer.

Overcoming is not for the future; it is a present-day thing. You can't become an overcomer unless you start overcoming these issues one by one today in your Now Moments. Only then will you be able to truly help the others in your path, a topic we will cover in the next chapter.

In Summary

Life is filled with obstacles. We grow by overcoming them, but our innate response to obstacles is to quit. That means we need an attitude adjustment to see us to the other side. One way to do that is to reframe obstacles and challenges. Another is to recognize that when you are at the bottom, the only place to go is upward. Finally, departmentalize your problems so they won't become one insurmountable mountain: this is the effective way to turn challenges into victories.

Practice

1. *Look at the challenges that you are facing today. Write them down as a scenario on a piece of paper. Now take a pen and circle each separate challenge. Take other sheets of paper and put each challenge on a separate sheet. You have now departmentalized your challenges.*

_____

_____

_____

_____

_____

_____

_____

_____

_____

_____

_____

2. *Envision a safe deposit box. Open it up and take out all the anger and resentments that you have placed there. Now envision that safe deposit box empty. What are you feeling?*

_____

_____

_____

_____

_____

_____

_____

_____

_____

_____

_____

_____

_____

_____

_____

_____

_____

_____

_____

_____

_____

_____

_____

_____

_____

_____

_____

_____

CHAPTER TEN

HELPING OTHERS

I have this saying, "Blessed people bless people." What I mean is that since we are always blessed, we can always be a blessing in giving to others. Unfortunately, people seem to be either givers or takers. Takers are in the mind frame of not having enough so they go and take it from somewhere else. They are always in need. Givers are always brimming and resourceful because they say, "What do I have to give?"

Givers are attracted to situations where they're able to give and, therefore, people are always giving to them. You'll see that happen with so many charities supported by companies and personalities where others see what they are doing and ask: "How can I help?"

There is a beautiful passage from the Bible: "As long as the earth endures, seedtime and harvest, cold and heat, summer and winter, day and night will never cease." Genesis 8:22. That's how the world has always cultivated itself. Everything starts with a seed. Helping others also starts with a seed.

We are here today because of the seed that was planted in our mothers, and the light that brought forth that humanity in the womb, and thus a living child. The same goes for the fruit and vegetables we eat. All of it starts with a seed, a capsule that has the ability to reproduce itself over time once placed in the right environment. When we see ourselves as givers or seeds of encouragement, we are able to affect our communities and the environment around us.

This mind-set allows us to make room in our homes for friends and family who are from out of town, who couldn't find a hotel to stay at. It helps us identify the food we store in our pantries that could be used to feed unexpected guests. As I grew up, I watched my parents feed other families from our own groceries. Our refrigerator was always packed with food. My mom cooked massive pots of great Bahamian dishes, like pigeon peas and rice. We'd have cupboards packed with twenty-pound rice bags, ten pounds of sugar, and boxes of cereal.

> WISDOM KEY
>
> FIRST <u>BELIEVE</u> YOU CAN MAKE A DIFFERENCE IN ORDER TO MAKE ONE BELIEVE YOU CAN AND YOU <u>WILL</u>

When I moved to California, a group of us would hang out at a buddy's house in Los Angeles. He was from Afghanistan. Whenever we visited, he would ask if we were hungry, but his kitchen was meager with food. This one time, he only had a half a chicken breast, an egg, a stalk of celery, half an onion, and a can of tomatoes. It just didn't appear to be sufficient to feed one person, let alone three people. It seemed like nothing compared to how I was raised.

We'd be playing music, and aromas would start coming from the kitchen. Forty-five minutes later, three of us would be sitting down to a delicious three-course meal.

It was always surprising how he did it. I believe it meant more to him than just physically making a meal. I knew that in some ways he was better than us because he understood the importance of being a giver. We may have come from more, but because of his past, he knew how to take little and make it much.

That's what being an encourager is all about. It's saying, "I know that even though I'm discouraged, I've still got enough courage to help somebody else. Even if I don't have love in my own life, I still have enough love to love somebody else. Even though I might have my own health challenges, I will look past that and still try to help others deal with theirs."

Saving the Starfish

Helping others does not have to be big. You don't have to start a movement or create a foundation. What you need to do is switch to a giver's mind-set and put it into action. Then every person you help will have a ripple effect in the world.

There was a man taking a morning walk on the beach. He saw that the tide washed up hundreds of starfish, and when it receded, the starfish were left behind. The tide was fresh, and the starfish were alive, but because of the morning sunrays, they would die there.

The man took a few steps toward the fish, picked one up, and threw it into the water. He did this repeatedly. Another man came up behind him. He couldn't understand what he was doing, so he asked, "What are you doing, sir? There are hundreds of starfish lying here. How many can you save? What difference does it make?"

Instead of yielding to his distraction, the man took a few more steps, took up another starfish, threw it in the water, and said, "It makes a difference to this one."

So, what difference are we making? Big or small, it does not matter. If everyone made a small difference, we'd end up with a big outcome.

A Family of Giving

I saw this giving spirit in my mother and father for years. They were already saints in heaven, as far as I'm concerned, for raising, loving and protecting thirteen children. Yet, even with overwhelming amounts of work and stress on their resources, my parents always had their doors open to everyone. There were always people in our home. The family joke was that we never had a family picture without somebody else in it.

Our home, which my father built from the ground up, was an incredible sanctuary and safe haven. People and kids in the neighborhood, as well as folks from our church, knew to come, because it was a place where they were served and encouraged.

People would visit our home on Christmas day, once their own Christmas festivities were over. I'm talking about two to three days of celebrating and having a great time. It was such a place of joy.

Now, we didn't have a lot of money, and because of this I sometimes wore hand-me-downs. My parents might not have been able to get new clothing for each kid all the time, nevertheless, we always looked our best. We simply took whatever the next items were as far as what fitted. I can honestly say that we were rich in ways that I find hard to believe. It was an extraordinary environment to grow up in.

My mom is now up in age, and she's still a giver. I remember telling her, "Mom, you can't help that old lady; you got your own back problems." You think she listened? No. She still went out there and picked up a heavy bag of groceries to give to a fellow senior citizen.

I think it's an extraordinary testimony that givers give, blessed people bless people, and that as long as the earth remains, as you sow, you will reap. Some people call it paying it forward. Some people call it karma. You can call it whatever you want. Here's what I can tell you: Encouragers are encouraged. Lovers love and are loved, peacemakers receive peace, and they become that which they give.

From Taker to Giver

Even though I grew up in a home of giving, I used to be a taker. Being twelve out of thirteen children, I had plenty of people I could go to in order to get whatever I wanted. If one said no, I had eleven other possibilities of getting a yes. At some point, I always got a yes. The only thing worse than being an only child is being the baby of a big family—you're certainly going to be self-absorbed.

WISDOM KEY

YOU HAVE
TO <u>GIVE</u>
IN ORDER
TO <u>RECEIVE</u>

I remember making a conscious decision as an adult, saying, "I don't want to be a taker. I don't want to fall on that side of the spectrum. I've got to figure this out. I've got to make this transition." I'm not going to say it was overnight, because it wasn't. It was over a period of time, and I'm still learning. I'm still perfecting what it means to be a servant, what it means to position myself to walk into a room and say, "What do I have to offer?" as opposed to, "What can these people or situation offer to me?"

I think life opens to you when you are open to giving to it. It is an extraordinary experience to know that you're blessed simply because you are a blessing. I have learned how to ignite my Now Season with encouragement and giving. Without question, I can't take credit for the majority of what I have come to experience in my life. I know that the majority of what I have is because of what my father and mother gave throughout the years, and what their mothers and fathers gave. Because of them, I am here today, and I am able to be a giver.

To be a giver is to celebrate life, to celebrate my Now Season and share it with others. That's why I wrote the lyrics to this song years ago, which became an anthem at my concerts over the years.

Celebrate

What I want to say is that you've touched my life in so many ways
Each moment that I breathe the more I see the you inside of me
Oh, love patiently kind the way you have touched my life
And now I want to give you my heart always until the end of time

I celebrate you celebrate me and you together forever
Oh, my love I'll follow you where you may lead
You are my destiny

I woke up just in time a brand-new day bright sunshine
Don't want to live this life alone no
So, I decided to come home that's when you welcomed me in your
heart there's not a greater friend your arms
Embraced around me the way it was meant to be

Want to celebrate the day you saved my life
Want to celebrate the way you've changed my mind
Want to thank you for the love that sets me free
Lord I will celebrate you for all eternity

Go the Extra Mile

Here's a sad truth. People may never give you credit for the little things you've done to help them along the way. They may never say thank you or come back and give you a hug. You may never be acknowledged for your consistency, faithfulness, love, or generosity. But I will tell you this: what you did for them made a big impact on their lives even if they don't know it. And even if the returns don't come from them, you will get it from another person, another situation, or another place.

WISDOM KEY

YOU CAN CHANGE THE OUTSIDE WORLD BY CHANGING YOUR INSIDE WORLD

This is so true of relationships. The best relationships are the ones that involve two people who care about the little things for one another on a consistent basis. It's not the big show off or the big hooray that keeps a marriage strong. It's the simple touch on the shoulder, a kiss, a hug, or just listening that makes a world of difference.

Even if you can't pinpoint all the details of what that person does for you, you still know that there's something about that person that makes you feel better about yourself and motivates you to make them feel better about themselves.

It's like the husband who came home with roses for his wife, and his daughter asked, "What are the flowers for?" He said that several of his coworkers were complaining about their wives and children today. He realized how lucky he was that after twenty years of marriage and raising a daughter for the last seventeen years, he still had nothing to complain about. I once heard about a couple celebrating their fiftieth wedding anniversary. The husband took out an old envelope and handed his wife back the love note she wrote him in the seventh grade!

Your opportunity puts itself in front of you because you have something that it needs—an orphan to a childless couple, a vacant office in an accounting firm to an unemployed CPA, a gang-infested community to a youth-impact community outreach program, or an available, single man to an available, single woman.

Whether you know it or not, we each are someone else's opportunity, because we have something in us that someone else needs. When you miss that moment, then you have caused someone to miss his or her opportunity. However, when you take the moment to meet the need, you become an asset to that need, and others will begin to seek you out for further opportunities to solve other similar issues.

One powerful way to help others is by doing it through your own community of support: your family, friends, church, or non-profit organization. In the next chapter, I will talk about communities of support and how to build and sustain them.

In Summary

The world in many ways breaks into two groups—the givers and the takers. If you are following The Now Way of Life, you will become a giver. You will understand that you have the ability to plant seeds of thoughtfulness and caring through your words and actions. You will see the little things that you can do on a daily basis to help those around you. Because you are blessed, you will be a blessing to others. This is an important legacy to hand down to your children, which they, in turn, will hand down to their children.

Practice

1. *Answer these questions from your heart:*

   • *What are you currently doing in your life that is helping others?*

   _____

   _____

   _____

   _____

   _____

   _____

- *How can you step up your game to help more?*

_____

_____

_____

_____

_____

_____

- *How do the things you do fit in with your purpose?*

_____

_____

_____

_____

_____

_____

_____

2. *Create a plan for this Now Season that incorporates how you will help others with specific actions.*

_____

_____

_____

_____

_____

_____

_____

_____

_____

_____

_____

_____

_____

_____

_____

CHAPTER ELEVEN

CREATING A COMMUNITY OF SUPPORT

A little boy walked into a pet store to buy a puppy. Five puppies came running to him, but one lagged behind. "What is wrong with that dog?" asked the boy. The shop owner explained that he was born without a hip socket and would always be lame. "That's the puppy I want," the boy responded.

"You really don't want to buy this little dog. He is never going to play with you like the other puppies," the man explained. To his surprise, the little boy reached down and rolled up his pant leg, revealing a crippled leg and metal brace. "Well, I don't run so well myself, and the little puppy will need someone who understands."

Like the little boy in the story surrounded himself with a puppy that he could relate to and that could relate to him, we too need to surround ourselves with people who understand us and will be that community of support for us, living in the now.

They can be family, friends, or mentors in our personal and professional lives. With the exception of family, we choose everyone else who ends up in our support system. Remember, the sum of our choices is basically who and what we are, and that certainly includes the people who surround us.

This is certainly true of children who need to see respect and affection between their parents. My own observation in counseling with couples is that too often men do not feel respected and women do not feel loved. Men sometimes struggle with showing affection, even with their own children, which can make it difficult for the children to treat them with the respect that they need. A man's feeling of honor comes from his children and his wife, but if they are not treating him with respect because he's not being affectionate, it can cause the entire system of support to fall apart.

In a marriage, both husband and wife can get the corner office at the workplace. They can also receive accolades from tons of people, but the one person they look to for support is the spouse. That's because it's the spouse that is closest to the heart, and therefore both words and action have the biggest impact. The two key elements for a healthy environment in a relationship are love and respect.

The Importance of Friends

Siri, the virtual assistant feature in iPhone, is the best friend and a polite teacher of a young autistic boy named Gus. Conversations with Siri teach Gus a thing or two about politeness and about how it is totally okay to have an opinion that is not welcomed by the society at large. She is, by far, the only friend in Gus's world that accepts him totally without any judgments. In fact, she is the one who got him to open up and talk. One of the conversations between Siri and Gus, at one point, melted Gus's heart and toned him down a little:

Gus asked Siri about some music suggestions, and when she gave him some, he snapped and said, "I don't like that kind of music!" At which, Siri, being the polite and friendly virtual assistant that she is, replied, "You're certainly entitled to your opinion." It mellowed down Gus a little bit, and softly he replied, "Thank you for that music, though."

> WISDOM KEY
>
> A FRIEND IS SOMEONE WHO LOVES AT ALL TIMES.

You know, God is relational, and He created us to be relational beings. Therefore, we were made with a need for relationships. Real friends make up a crucial element of our community of support and are very different from family. Your family is chosen for you, and you don't have a say in the matter. But with friends, it's usually a mutual selection.

Affirmation – "Emotional Support or Encouragement"

I believe friendships are important because they are the relationships that bring about that uncommon affirmation—the assertion of truth—which I think is a fundamental component that all human beings need in life. It is absolutely crucial that you understand the importance of friends, and that should never take the place of anything else.

WISDOM KEY

FAMILY, LOVE, AND FRIENDSHIP ARE VITAL INGREDIENTS TO <u>HEALTHY LIVING</u>

I think about the different friendships that I've had throughout the years and how they have affirmed me. In every true friendship, there was a real affirmation of whatever it was that I was looking to do and accomplish. It was because of close friends that I was able to launch out into the deep and make power moves, as it pertains to my career and business. In the early part of my life, it was because of a close friend that I pursued my college degree. I really believe that I wouldn't have gone to college if it had not been for that specific person in my life who took the time and literally walked me through that process, encouraged me, and pointed me in the right direction.

If you think about it long enough, you would remember different critical moments in your life when there was a real friend who said just the right words, gave just enough encouragement, and provided sufficient affirmation that got you over and actually saved the outcome of where your life was headed.

In truth, many times our family may be challenged with our future choices and changes in life simply because they know more of our past than the average friend. They are all too familiar with our weaknesses, our infirmities, and our disconnects, if you will. Therefore, it's harder for them to sometimes see our greater possibilities, and it's difficult for them to see our impact when it comes to what we present to the world, to our generation, and our purpose. Unlike the brother or the aunty who may sometimes judge you by your past mishaps, a real friend is kind of like the blind supporter. They will simply accept, at face value, what you now exhibit and embrace you for who you are. They won't care about what used to be, what didn't happen, or your past mistakes. They genuinely encourage who you are, what you're presenting, and what you're about.

Real friendships are a safe place for communication. You can say what you need to say in the way that you need to say it, and in the way that you know that it's going to be accepted. Once it's spoken, a real friend usually knows what you meant by it and what is said won't be misinterpreted. Most importantly, the information is not going to be shared. But rather, they protect your information and don't judge or expose it. A real friend takes your secrets to the grave.

If you have someone who is leaking and littering your secrets here and there when they get upset, or releasing them in an environment that they know will bring possible damage, that's not a genuine friend. We all need that genuine friendship where we are able to share and expose our thoughts in a healthy way and in a healthy environment that will allow us to release those endorphins—to relinquish those thoughts from our minds into a place where there can be some balance. Let's face it, sometimes our thoughts are not balanced and our opinions about things can be a little off, but a good friend can help steer us the right way and will talk us off the ledge if need be.

There are some people in your life who will push you into a fight or coerce you into breaking up your marriage. A sincere friend will say, "Let's rationally try to fix this; let's try to find balance here. You're being too hostile; you're being too impatient." They know enough to not push you too hard, know when to be quiet and allow you to talk, and when to speak up and say, "Ok, I got to say something right here."

Real friends will work out anything and work through anything no matter how difficult because there's enough grace on both sides that says, "It's time to squash this; it's time to let this go. It's time to bounce back from that, clear the slate, and keep it encouraged." So, when it comes to the importance of friends, you must know that they matter a great deal and are vital in the life of a person who is looking to walk in real success and looking to have a life of purpose and destiny.

It's so important that when all others have failed and even when you have failed, you have that friend who is just going to walk with you through it. We are responsible for them, and they're responsible for us. This responsibility is very different than our responsibility to our children, spouse, or boss.

Friends Are From All Walks Of Life

Friendships are initiated from different periods of life, like high school, college, or through your travels to other countries. Some people are blessed enough to have childhood friends that last all throughout their lifetime, or what they call friends from "the womb to the tomb." I know a few people who have that, and I can gratefully say that I have been blessed with a few of those lifetime friends, too. I do have some friends from high school, but my real, close friends certainly came from my college experience, and they are still my friends to this day. I must say though, that along this journey, I've met some even greater friends, and even closer ones in my adulthood—friends who you just know are God connections because of the support they bring to your life, and you just want to support them back. Friends who you know will endure for a lifetime.

Friends Are There For a Reason

Real friendship lets you pick up at the same place where you left off even if you haven't seen each other in years. It should equal out to 50/50. In other words, the bill they're running up on you is the same bill you're running up on them. Sometimes you have it, sometimes they do; sometimes they are down, and other times they will have to be that shoulder for you. So it becomes a partnership, if you will. One that is so enriching that even though it costs you, it is also an investment that you can get dividends on. If it's a real friendship, you will be able to pull from it many times.

I often say, "Be careful of using the term 'friend' so quickly." That's a title that should be kept and reserved for those who have that track record in your life. There are acquaintances and colleagues that you can have, and people that you just know and are associated with, for example, your neighbors. But when it comes to a real friend, that's someone who loves at all times and is there till the end—whether it be the end of life or the end of a particular season in your life.

Keeping Your Community of Support

Looking back at my younger years, I can now see how it would've been wise to take a second or two before saying certain things or challenging some situations that could've just worked themselves out on their own. It would've been wiser to just simply ask myself, "Will my words create a better or worse environment of support?" Instead of pushing my point and being right, I would've stopped and questioned whether my actions would cause loss and put a strain on a very close-knit, strong support system or would they strengthen it.

I'm not talking about compromising or putting up with something that you shouldn't have to put up with. It's not so much what you say, but how you say it. It's the words you choose to make your point and the tone of your expression. Your delivery can either create an awesome support system or it can literally crush it.

We all know someone who got married and stopped being a good friend because they got so caught up in their new life. In some way, this is understandable, but if the marriage hits a rough patch and that person goes looking for the friend, he or she may find that the friend has moved on. It's so important that you keep all those meaningful relationships intact and find balance to all of it. Obviously, you can't act like a single person anymore once you're married, but remember, a friend loves at all times.

The same is true about spouses; we submit to one another and love one another as God loves us. And we are to honor our parents no matter what. Nobody's parents are perfect, but we are still to honor them. All of that will create such an extraordinary community of support.

Our Children

Our children are part of our community of support, and no matter what, they are our responsibility. We don't get credit for taking care of our kids; it's the least we can do. No matter how old or rebellious they get, always let them know you're there for them and will never give up on them. Hopefully, these same children will turn around and take care of you when you become old.

As a parent, it was very important to me to make wise decisions to create a safe and structured environment of growth for my son, so he could feel secure and thrive. I had to decide on the right place to live, the right school for him to attend, and so on. You may have experienced similar choices for your children. I couldn't just grab the first place that became available for rent. I had to research the crime rates for the areas and make comparisons between schools.

Looking for ways and means of stretching the almighty dollar is also something we always find ourselves doing as parents: not only diversifying economically in all that we do, but being sincere on how we're going to leave an inheritance for our children's children. In doing this, we should also consider spending time with them so they can learn how to balance a checkbook, understand the family business, and learn about family-owned properties. If you only have one child, what are you doing to prepare him or her to take things on, if something suddenly happens, God forbid, unexpectedly?

Sometimes we are so focused on being such good providers for our children that we forget other very important bonding factors, like taking them to our workplace so it's not such a mysterious place, and sitting down with them and talking about our day, as well as theirs.

One of the concerns that has often come up in counseling is favoritism. We see this in adults who carry a lot of issues that they are harboring because they think a parent favored the other sibling. Here's what I tell them. Parents do have favorites, even if they don't know it. Favorite, however, doesn't mean that they favor one kid over the other. It means that one child will probably get a little bit more than the other one simply because he or she is there more—always checking in and/or providing support to the parent's needs.   Somebody on the outside may look at that as favoritism. But, in reality, it's about how much a child is involved with the support system of honoring his or her parents.

There is also a need to support children who don't necessarily have the personalities that fit the upbringing of your household. Some of our kids are like us, and some are very much the opposite of us. They each have their pros and cons, but, all in all, if there is a gap or a difference between us as parents and the child, it's ok to express and embrace the difference. I believe that the essential thing when it comes to our support system, as it pertains to our children, is communication.

The effort of communication is so important because sometimes it's not just about giving advice—which all good parents want to do—but it's really about being able to be an ear to listen or a shoulder to lean on. We find that many

WISDOM KEY

DON'T GET <u>RID</u> OF YOUR <u>FRIENDS</u> JUST BECAUSE YOU GET MARRIED

times in our own lives, as children, we were one person at school and a different person at home, because the opportunity for self-expression was not there most of the time. It is important for our children to feel that it's safe to be themselves at home. That doesn't mean we have to be their best friend—children definitely need parents to be parents. What it means is that we continue to be loving yet authoritative, while creating an atmosphere with great communication.

The ability to communicate in a healthy environment with our children, and our children with us, is necessary in cultivating a great support system. We know there has to be a lot of guidance and correction, a lot of regulating and that kind of thing. But there should also be a consistent time of letting our guards down, letting our hair down, to be able to smile and create opportunities for there to be laughter amongst our children. If the family is not athletic, then a movie will suffice or just spending time in the park walking or simply finding something that will take us out of our usual environment and schedule—something that lends the opportunity for there to be joy and peace in our amusement. I think it is so needed that as we grow older we have memories of our kids laughing and smiling and that they have those memories of us, too. It's tough to hear people say, "I've never seen my father laugh or crack a joke," or, "I've never seen my mother once dance or skip around."

WISDOM KEY

GROW <u>OLD</u> WITH THE PEOPLE WHO REALLY KNOW YOU AND STILL <u>LIKE</u> YOU

Cultivating the right atmosphere and allowing it to be a part of their childhood experience will strengthen that support and connection years down the road. Marla Gibbs, the great actress who played the famous character Florence Johnston on the hit TV show *The Jeffersons* back in her younger years, once told an incredible story. She's now well into her eighties, and when she received an award, she said something I will never forget.

She said, "Be nice to your children when they are young, and when they are older, they may give you a job." At 80 plus years old, Florence Johnson was still a working actress.

She was hired by her own daughter, who became a producer and director.

This really sums up the whole concept of what it really means to invest in your children, making sure that the support system is there because you definitely will need it, and they will, too. I look at my own mom, who's currently being challenged with Alzheimer's disease; she not only has one child, but she has twelve that take the time to care for her needs around the clock.

Get Involved

Another way to build your community of support is to get involved with others. Earlier in this book, I talked about new mothers getting together to support each other and how vital that is to making it through the rewarding but hard season of newborns. There was this young father, whose name is Jake, who received sole custody of his 3-week-old son because the mother was unable to care for the baby. Imagine being the father of a tiny baby, having sole custody of this child, but not knowing how to hold your child securely or where to turn for support. Like most new parents, Jake had many questions and concerns, so he turned to a non-profit foundation that gives help to people who are entering parenthood and need support. He attended their Infant Wellness Class and learned about normal infant behavior and when to call the doctor. He worked with their *Man2Man* mentors to understand his role as a father and to gain parenting skills. They also taught him basic baby care along with life skills, which gave Jake much-needed confidence as a new dad.

Jake was able to get the tools that would help him thrive and succeed as a new father. This is just one example of how important it is to connect to a healthy community system that can help carry you through a challenging time. Like the Man2Man support program, there are so many other ways to build your community while helping others in need: local after-school programs, Girl Scouts, ministries, or a women's club. The list goes on and on and changes depend on what Now Season you are in.

Finally, connecting with causes that are bigger and greater than you will end up not only fulfilling so much great purpose in your life, but it will also become an extraordinary support system for others in need.

Not Forgetting as Your Season Changes

Support systems are crucial in our Now Seasons, but it's vital that as our seasons change, our support systems change with them. Life is very seasonal, and so, although it's important, it can be difficult to move from one system to the next. For example, there were people in my life who were phenomenal in certain seasons, but we were not able to stay connected in other seasons of my life.

Essentially, there are those who are connected to me now that would have not been connected to me back then, simply because we would have been in two different spaces and with opposite mind-sets. Still, I do believe that there are a few people who can transition with you through just about every season, and when it's all said and done, if you're lucky, you might end up with two or three really good friends who have walked with you and have your back through every season of your life. Three is actually a big number, because it's about one or two people who can go through it all with you and still remain the same.

As your season changes, your community of support will change. Your family and real friends will move with you

---—∞—---

WISDOM KEY

IF YOU'RE NOT READY TO <u>GIVE</u>, YOU'RE NOT READY TO BE IN A <u>RELATIONSHIP</u>

---—∞—---

through those seasons, just as you will move with them through their seasons. Sometimes those changes will test your support system in ways that you don't anticipate, like the elderly couple in this relationship:

"An elderly man hurried to his 8:00am doctor's appointment, he wanted to finish quickly so that he could get to another appointment. The doctor asked what it was, and the old man proudly said that every morning at 9:00am he would go to the hospital and have breakfast with his wife. The doctor asked what her condition was, and he replied that for the past 5 years his wife has had Alzheimer's and hasn't known who he is. The doctor asked the old man why he continued to visit her if she had no idea who he was anymore…and the old man replied…"Because I still know who she is."

This story is a perfect example of what it means to continue on in love no matter the difficult changes that may come to your relationship. At one point, this man's wife was probably the one cooking the breakfast, cleaning the house, and giving warm, affectionate hugs. But now, because of her illness, she was unable to do much of anything, much less remember who he was. In spite of the change and the challenges, he still found it in his heart to turn the tables and support his wife, even if that meant just spending time with her. In life, your seasons will definitely go through many changes, but there has to be a fight and a faith that says, "I

WISDOM KEY

ASK YOURSELF THE RIGHT QUESTIONS FIRST BEFORE ASKING THEM OF THE PERSON YOU'RE LOOKING TO MARRY

---

still believe in the reason I committed to this system in the first place." Remember, whatever it was that gave you the strength and will to start that union of support, you still have it in you. It just may need to be redirected in a different manner for a new purpose. That's living in your Now no matter how it may change.

Because of the constant changes in our seasons, you have what I call seasonal support systems. These are partnerships you develop with the people whose paths you've crossed—people with a common goal, with like visions, and similar things that they are trying to accomplish within that time. This is why I believe that the full-time student fares better being on campus at a university as opposed to the part-time student attending community college., simply because they are around a support system of like-minded people more often.

It's important that we recognize the people who are there to support us; however, it is very common to have a support system and not know it. Because if you don't know it and can't recognize it, you may end up losing it or not taking advantage of it in the way that you should. Taking advantage of our support system doesn't mean that we should manipulate or abuse it, but to simply recognize and embrace that, "This is where I am, this is who I'm connected to, and these are the people who can give me the opportunity to do x, y and z, and who I can give the chance to do what needs to be done for them in their Now Season."

I'm reminded of a young couple who had a premature baby. When I went to show support and help bring guidance and encouragement to them, I found that they had connected with other couples who also had premature babies. If you know anything about this process, there is a high percentage and a great risk of health issues with these types of babies. The sad reality is that many of them don't make it. It was important for this couple to have that support group of like-minded parents who were going through the same ordeal. This unique group of parents kept each other encouraged. They had to keep one another lifted up, celebrating all the little milestones—even if it was as simple as the baby passing gas or being able to pee for the first time. I discovered from this process that the simple, insignificant things to us were huge milestones to these little champions and warriors and therefore brought a ripple of celebration and encouragement to the parents in that support system.

We see the same thing with veterans and people who have experienced trauma and have witnessed death firsthand. Because of this common challenge, they too can understand what it means to try overcoming such tragedies. Prior to their current season and support systems, I would imagine the parents would probably have told you that a group consisting of parents with premature babies would have never been their group of choice to hang with, at least not until they too found themselves in that same situation.

As you go through this life's journey, be careful to listen and keep your eyes open, because your seasons will tell you who your support systems are, the people that God has placed in your life to help you. These are people who are ready to support you, but if you are too prideful or disconnected, you may miss the opportunity to get the help that you need. There are also times in your life where you'll find that you are the most accomplished person in the circle of people around you or whomever you're connected to. That season will let you know that this is the time to pour into others, help some people, or point some people in the right direction. If you're not careful, you'll miss the opportunity to change somebody's life.

In Summary

A community of support could be made up of your family, friends, or neighbors. Some you chose to have, and others are chosen for you. Regardless of who they are, a community of support thrives on reciprocal relationships. You support them, they support you. One of the most cherished groups within your community of support is real friends who have a long history with you. It is vital that you nourish those relationships and learn to watch your words and actions so that they do not tear the fiber of your support network. At the end of the day, learn how to embrace yourself no matter what because you are the center of your community of support, and you're always there.

Practice

1. *Make a list of all the people in your community of support. Include your family, friends, organizations, and mentors.*

_____

_____

_____

_____

_____

_____

2. *Create two columns. In the first column, write down how that person provides you with support. In the second column, write down how you provide that person with support.*

_____

_____

_____

_____

_____

_____

_____

_____

_____

_____

_____

_____

3. *Review the columns. Does it seem balanced to you? Should you be asking for more support or giving more support? Understand that things do not need to be balanced; they vary from season to season. However, you should be aware.*

CHAPTER TWELVE

THE RIGHT ATTITUDE IN YOUR NOW

Attitude is one of the most underrated characteristics in everyday life. We don't understand how important it is for our progression and success. Attitude is the energy of successful living, but it can also be to your demise. It is the position of your mind in action. Attitude is acting out how you think, and how you think is what you act out.

No matter how much you've accomplished, how much you walk in purpose, or how much you believe in something bigger in your life, if your attitude is negative, your everyday life will be negative. You could have an extraordinary day, but because your attitude about the day is negative, what you see and experience will be negative.

Do you remember the story of the fox and the grapes? A fox saw a juicy bunch of grapes hanging from a branch. He licked his lips, jumped, and missed. Again and again he tried. Finally, he turned up his nose and walked away, saying, "They were probably sour anyway."

Do you have a sour-grapes attitude? Instead, how about replacing it with an attitude of gratitude? Gratitude is the quality of being thankful with the readiness to show joy in the goodness of something. It's important that you have a mind that's going to act thankful. When you start talking about having the right attitude, it's about being positive, joyful, and happy with an expectation that greater things will happen. After all, the root of "happiness" is "happen."

It All Starts with You

Here's a truth I have learned: people will *not* see in you what you cannot see in yourself. Rarely will an individual see something about you that you are not feeling about yourself. It all starts with you. That means you cannot go through life reacting to life; instead, you have to act and allow life to react to you.

Often, we look outward for something to adjust our attitude and make us happy. This is a false narrative that many of us believe in: we expect our encounters with people, situations, relationships, and jobs to make us happy. We presume that someone else will adjust our attitude and our perception of how we see life and ourselves.

WISDOM KEY

ATTITUDE
REALLY DOES
DETERMINE
ALTITUDE

Then we are disappointed when we realize that these encounters have done nothing to help us.

You, however, have the power to change your attitude to one of positivity and gratitude. If you travel through life with a positive attitude, then experiences can become positive. It will not matter if something is a good or bad challenge. It will not matter if you are rich or poor. It will not matter where you live. It will not matter if what you are doing is exciting or boring. If you *choose* to be positive, the situation will have a much higher chance of being positive, and hence, you will create your own opportunity to live in a positive Now Moment.

Positioning Your Mind

The first step is to believe in where you're going, as opposed to what you're going through. Many people have a strong belief that they'll get through something. It's okay, obviously, to believe you're going to get through something. But what if you actually start time traveling in your mind and go beyond your current circumstance, situation, dilemma, or whatever it may be. It's better if you think, "Not only am I going to get through this, but here's where I'm going to get to. Once this is all done, this is what I'm really striving for."

One way to accomplish this change of attitude is to envision the outcome before you begin. Envision how it's going to end before you take a job, get into a relationship, decide to raise children, or do a business deal. If you envision the ending before you begin, it gives you a reference point of how your attitude should be positioned.

When things get tough, go back to your original vision. Go back to how you originally believed you would get through a situation and the end result. This keeps you on the right trajectory with the right attitude. Do this while positioning your mind for a positive outcome no matter what.

Championship athletes do this all of the time. They always talk about how they envision winning. They envision what they are going to do and how they are going to do it. Some have specific plans while others are vaguer. What is consistent with all of them is the attitude to win—the attitude to say, "This will be a positive outcome even if the odds are stacked against me."

The second thing about attitude and gratitude is that we have to allow good information to transform our mind. We can't just study to achieve success, but we have to study to change our mind. As you're reading a book, let it transform the way you think. Let it transform the way you perceive things. And let it transform your attitude about things. I make this mistake all the time; I'm always reading stuff and sharing it with others or using it to fix a problem. But often I don't use it to transform myself.

Change vs. Transformation

As you're reading this book, not only are you reading the information, but you're also allowing the information to transform how you look at life. You are using it to help you perceive what you're going through so you don't stay the same. One of the things that is so important to understand about transformation is that it is a huge part of your success plan. It is a huge part of going from good to great and from almost to uttermost.

It's one thing to change; it's another thing to transform. You can change addresses and still be the same person. You can bring the same junk and put it in a new house, and you'll still have the same problems and the same mess. But you can take the same house and transform it. You can completely change what's in there, remodel, clean it up, and put in new furniture, the whole nine yards.

—⚬—

WISDOM KEY

A SMILE
PRECEDING WORDS
CAN OPEN
MANY DOORS

—⚬—

Nobody's telling you to take on a new mind. You're only going to have one mind; you're not going to get a new brain in this lifetime. It's the same brain, but what you're doing is spring cleaning. You're taking some things out, and you're putting some new things in. And you're allowing it to literally think a whole different way.

Attitude is all about how you think. It's all about how you perceive things and take action. So not only do I think it, but I act as I think. You can't tell me you have joy if you're acting like you're upset or sad. You can't tell me you're hopeful if every way that you're acting out is hopeless. That means your attitude is not a hopeful attitude; it's a hopeless attitude.

Don't be a Victim

When it comes to having that right attitude of gratitude and success, you don't position yourself as a victim. You can't have false hope, because false hope leads to false results. But you have to understand that no matter what you are going through, you're not a victim because of it. In fact, it's an opportunity to be victorious. You can't be a champion unless you have something to champion. You can't be a winner unless you have a fight in front of you. You can't overcome something unless there is something to overcome.

Don't ask the question "Why me?" Ask the question – "Why not me?" This is the dialogue in your mind: "I can take this. I can endure this. This is the challenge that is exactly for me. This will take me to that next level in my life that will give me the results that I really need for this season in my life."

When I launched my own company, I went from only having to do my job to running an entire business. I was responsible for finance, sales, marketing, and operations. Every time something unexpected would happen, I'd feel like a failure or questioned if I had made a huge mistake starting my company. Illogically, I would even feel like something was done to me, even though I had made the choice to go out on my own and not collect a paycheck anymore.

I had to realize that sometimes you don't balance the books right. Sometimes an idea is not as good as you think. Some shows you'll put on won't draw people. Whatever the situation was, I had to look at it as an opportunity to grow. I had to have the attitude that this was an opportunity to revamp, restructure, and move forward. Thinking and acting like a victim was not an option.

If you don't have an attitude of victimization, then you're never victimized, no matter the situation. You actually are a victor. This is not something that's easy or can be done overnight. Instead, think of it as attitude adjustments that you can do on a consistent basis. Think of it like taking care of a car. Any car needs a tune-up, oil changes, and gas. But first your attitude has to be that you will do what it takes to keep that car running well and then putting it into action.

A Positive Attitude Leads to Opportunities

Many years ago, two salesmen were sent by a British manufacturer to Africa to investigate and report back on a potential market for selling shoes. The first salesman reported back, "There is no potential here: nobody wears shoes." Just then the other salesman reported back, "There is massive potential here: nobody wears shoes."

Both made the same observation, but each had a different perspective on what they saw. Likewise, in life, we may all see the same thing but perceive it differently. Perspective is the position you take or the attitude you have about how you see something.

There are folks out there who are walking through life blindly with a hit-or-miss attitude. They have no care for the opportunity to be able to see what's really going on around them. They've missed the child in need, overlooked the problem in their neighborhood that really needed to be addressed, and looked past issues in their own family that would've probably opened the door to a new business that would've helped the next generation.

WISDOM KEY

MOTIVATION GIVES YOU <u>ENERGY</u>, AND ENERGY <u>MOTIVATES</u> YOU

Every obstacle we come across gives us an opportunity to improve our circumstances. Having a positive attitude allows you to take advantage of that opportunity, which is essentially finding a need and meeting it. That's what a good opportunist does, and that's the sole way to stop anyone from taking your opportunity. But how can you meet a need if you have not made the decision to look for one? You will never find something you are not looking for. If we begin to open our eyes and look with intention, we will begin to see a world of possibilities that surrounds us. We will begin to see the open doors that are waiting for us to walk through.

Think, Act and Speak Like a Winner

In many ways, life echoes what we sound off, and that sound can be literally in our attitudes: our facial expressions, our actions, and what we say. If you think, act, and speak as a winner, life will open up opportunities for you to have victory. When you think, act, and speak as a loser, life will respond to you as though you are defeated.

This is why it is important to understand who you are and the power you have to win. This is something you can start today and begin to walk in right now. When you do, it will become a domino effect, causing things to start falling into place victoriously for your life.

You are almost to the end of this book. I'd like to conclude with a chapter about how you can immediately activate The Now Way of Life. I want to show you how to do it now.

In Summary

You have the choice to control your attitude. You can choose to be negative or positive. People, places, and things cannot make you a happy person if your attitude is one of negativity and defeat. Conversely, you can elevate difficult situations and challenges by assuming an attitude of positivity. To truly change your attitude, you need to transform your mind.

Practice

1. *Think of the last three difficult situations in your life. Did you face them with an attitude of negativity or positivity? Write down what you did and what you would now do differently based on what you have read in this book.*

_____

_____

_____

_____

_____

_____

_____

_____

_____

_____

_____

_____

_____

_____

_____

_____

_____

_____

CHAPTER THIRTEEN

DO IT NOW

I'm often baffled by the question, "Where does my inner drive come from?" It's a question I get often from young people. If I had to sum it up, I would say my inner strength comes from a series of *small acts* that have shaped and morphed into strength beyond what I could ever come up with on my own.

This realization has led me to believe that one important element of *The Now Way of Life* is to be aware and act on the belief that small things in our life matter as much as bigger things. Acting on the smaller things is what keeps us moving when we are stuck or overburdened.

Let me give you an example from my own life. There was a time when, after years of singing on major stages around the world and being in the studio with different bands, I found myself in a slump. I thought that portion of my life was over, and I had maxed out my career as a musician. Oddly enough, I didn't even recognize it as a slump; I just accepted it as the next season in my life.

It wasn't until the mother of one of my best friends told me one day after lunch that I had what it takes to make it big. It caught me so off guard that I asked her, "Are you serious? Do you really believe that?"

She answered, "Absolutely." I never forgot that moment. Her compliment re-ignited something in me, and that became the day that I began to change my perception of my future and the plans I needed to make for my life. It was a little thing, that conversation, but it played a very big part in my life.

Life is often a canvas for big occasions. Senior prom, the first car and home, graduations, marriage, births, and deaths are the major events we remember for a lifetime. But here's a truth: recognizing the little things all around us often focuses us on what matters most. Small things anchor us and allow us to live fully in the Now and bring depth to our past.

WISDOM KEY

LITTLE ACTS OF LOVE MATTER WHEN WE LEAST EXPECT IT

Throughout this book, I've told you a bit about my mom. Today as I watch her struggle with Alzheimer's, I want to hear every word she says. I am not looking for big thoughts or profound ideas. I just want to be able to hear her voice as she begins to lose the ability to have clear thoughts. Every word and syllable have become so valuable to my family. Spending time with her is a vital part of my Now Season, even as I travel the world teaching, performing, and producing.

And it's not only family members who have that impact with small things. Do you remember that second-grade teacher who believed in you or the music teacher who lifted your day by playing your favorite songs? I do. For me, it was a combination of all those people in my childhood who helped me formulate such a big imagination about who I could be. I didn't know then, but their words, smiles, and unwillingness to judge me built such confidence and endurance.

There are so many people in our lives who do small things that we fail to appreciate. And because we are so often not in our Now Moment, we also fail to appreciate the things we have. When I moved to California, I was shocked at how much colder the beaches were than in South Florida. I remember thinking, "You've got to be kidding me! I no longer have the luxury of just going to the beach and jumping into warm, clear water?" It made me think about the hundreds of days each year that I failed to go swimming in Florida. Something that was so minute and seemingly irrelevant at the time now took center stage in my social life.

We forget small things too often. Right now, your best friend is standing next to you, the love of your life is living just up the street, and someone wants to make the best offer you'll ever get for some old object sitting in your home or garage. Are you blowing off connecting because you think you will do it later? My friend, it's the little things in life that make up the big difference when it's all said and done. And doing it later is a poor substitute for doing it now.

Get Off the Sidelines

You don't have to hold back, you don't have to carry things on for long periods of time, and you don't have to wait for your dreams and goals to come to reality in order to snatch yourself out of that place of stagnancy.

Some people think that once they find the right person, they will address the issue of loneliness. What they may not realize is that you can still be lonely even with the right person. Others think that once they have the right amount of money, they will become a better businessperson. But if you can't budget a hundred dollars, you won't be able to budget thousands of dollars. The way you graduate to budgeting your thousands is by being accountable for your tens and hundreds.

The same applies to relationships, careers, and your psychological makeup. It's just a matter of identifying your issues, acknowledging that the challenge is there, and then saying to yourself, "I will begin to address it now."

When we sit at the sidelines of our challenges and don't attempt to do anything, then we are silently declaring that we've lost. This was one of the reasons why World War II, which involved Hitler and the Nazi army, took place. After his election into the political arena, Adolf Hitler began to lay the foundations of the Nazi state. Guided by racism and authoritarian principles, the Nazis eradicated individual freedoms and decreed the creation of a Volk Community, a society that would, in theory, transcend class and religious differences.

So many of the neighboring countries thought that the problem was going to subside and that, at some point, Hitler was going to be defeated by someone else. But little did they know that by them doing nothing, this one man would brew contention that would soon develop into one of the biggest wars —World War II.

The more they sat back and did nothing, the more ground Hitler gained, as he took over territory after territory and became a huge force that had the possibility to literally take over all of Europe. To quote one of the forces that took England off of the sidelines, Winston Churchill: "If you're going through hell, keep going."

Lazy, Late, or Just Not Looking

There are three other big reasons why people don't move on and therefore miss great opportunity: they are late, lazy, or just not looking for them.

Many of us have become couch potatoes as we fail to actively pursue life's prospects, despite our abilities to carry out the challenges that we take on. We are just too lazy to go the extra mile. I don't know many successful people alive today in any genre who did not have to work tirelessly to get where they are. People with real significance make up in their mind, "I'm going to burn the midnight oil and stay up late to make sure I meet my deadlines."

We have more people today in our society who want to take the easy route. They want to spend the least amount of money to make it happen, use the least amount of time getting it done, and do the least amount of work to see it through. Putting in the work will essentially get us closer to that next level. As the poet Henry Wadsworth Longfellow wrote, "The heights by great men reached and kept were not attained by sudden flight, but they, while their companions slept, were toiling upward in the night."

Additionally, in many areas of our lives, we've become people who are always late. We arrive late for the party, so we miss that network connection that could have landed us a big contract. We are late in submitting our assignments, so our final grades are lower. We are late in saying that we are sorry or in showing love. It's one of the biggest challenges we all face, one most of us opt out of fixing.

When you stop being late and start showing up on time, it changes the outcome drastically. Being on time shows not only that you care but also that you have respect for what you are about to encounter. If you can be punctual, you implicitly acknowledge that you value other people's limited time.

Getting to a meeting or an appointment on time shows that it's important to you and something for which you've planned. Being chronically late, on the other hand, sends the message that whatever you're doing is simply more important than the task at hand. And when that happens, people who were interested in giving you a good opportunity may turn and give it to the person who's on time, ready, and excited to take it to the next level.

Great possibilities are found in every opportunity you encounter; how you use them will determine the level of greatness. For example, when you decide to seize the moment to audition for a part, it may not look like it will bring you fame. Yet when you take the challenge, as it unfolds, you will see the true potential it has to evolve itself into something extraordinary.

As much as we all want to not prolong the time it takes to be successful, it does require time. Instant results don't last, especially if you don't have the discipline to maintain what it really takes to sustain it. Discipline only comes when you indulge yourself in the process of hard work, consistency, and endurance.

I'm not knocking cutting the corners here or there to get to some results in a quicker way. All I'm saying is that real success takes real work, and real work means you can't be lazy. You can start the journey of tapping into your opportunities by making the effort. When you do, you will secure the foundation of what it is you really want to achieve.

Don't Wait for Victory

Not waiting for victory allows you to be successful in many areas of your life, achieving set goals and taking advantage of good and bad situations, no matter how hard it gets. This type of success is not only reflected in completing the final lap of college and attaining that degree. It can also be seen in picking up the pieces from being a high school dropout and getting that GED so you can be on your way to college.

It's not just maintaining that big title in the law firm where you work, it's having a no-quit attitude every time you get turned down, stepped on, or thrown out from that which you so earnestly work toward. Not waiting for victory means accepting the fact that you are victorious now and that you already have the ability to win no matter what comes your way. Former NASA astronaut Jim Lovell once said: "There are people who make things happen, those who watch things happen, and then those who wondered what happened."

Victory is not something to wait for. No army that wants to win will sit and do nothing with the expectation that their enemy will soon surrender. Instead, they will plan for victory, seek it out, and fight for it. Can you imagine a group of soldiers sitting down, just several hundred yards away from their enemy's camp, twiddling their fingers while hoping that their enemies will drop dead so they can win the battle? They are be in for a rude awakening, because those enemies are about to run them over with ease.

So it is with our own lives. When we do nothing and wait for things to happen, we set ourselves up to fail big. Michael Jordan's passion for basketball, which led him to become an international icon, legend, all-time hero of the NBA, and the greatest athlete of his generation, led him to not wait for victory. When Jordan was inducted into the NBA Hall of Fame in 2009, he gave a speech about how he got cut from his high school basketball team, became motivated, and then went on to become a great player in the NBA.

In that speech, he talked about the 1985 All-Star Game freeze-out, where jealous older players supposedly stopped passing him the ball. He talked about Pat Riley, a coach who turned basketball into wrestling every time his team played Jordan, and recounted every remark that someone made that could turn into an insult against him. He flew Leroy Smith, the player who replaced him on the varsity team, and Pop Herring, the coach who "cut" him, in for the ceremony. He thanked them all, because he realized a long time ago that his friends made him good, but his enemies made him great.

It's a huge mistake to wait for victory in any area or season of your life, because to wait for victory is to walk in defeat. When you walk in defeat, you allow your challenging situations to beat you down without fighting back. You give up on the dreams that you dream and fail to make plans to mobilize them. You even stop believing in yourself. When you wait to win, you become disengaged, idle, and nonchalant. As a result, life runs you over or passes you by.

> **WISDOM KEY**
>
> TODAY YOU CAN OVERCOME ANYTHING IF YOU'LL STOP LOOKING FOR THE BIG CONNECTION AND START THE SMALL CHANGES IN YOUR LIFE

It's important to make up in your mind that in your Now Season, you are victorious, a winner, and an overcomer. Do this before you face your challenges—and maintain that mentality as you go through them. You have to determine that you have what it takes and that you are going to get through whatever it is that you are going through. You need to take on this mentality, because being a defeated person will inevitably cause you to compromise in many areas of your life.

Walking in defeat is a mind-set that affects how you approach everyday life. It also affects how you deal with people. If you think that you are already defeated, then you will soon start to feel that way, which ultimately will cause you to start giving up on things and people who are valuable and priceless. You may even find yourself not wanting to fight for your own life and all the good it still has to offer.

Mom's Story

Throughout this book, I have shared the stories of my own life as well as parables that have special meaning to me. I'd like to conclude with a story about my mom, the woman who told her scared 17-year-old son, "Everything is going to be alright. Keep going forward."

For many years I've watched the passion, time, and care she put into preparing and presenting meals for our family. She carefully and thoroughly washed the vegetables she picked from her own garden. Meats were properly cleaned, chopped, seasoned, and left to marinate for at least a day or two before cooking a Thanksgiving or Sunday meal. She took the time to allow peas to boil, instead of getting them from a can, and her spices and vegetables were specially selected to create the right flavor and consistency.

Mom's cooking released delightful aromas that permeated our whole home. Her food literally pulled on your sense of smell and brought your taste buds alive from afar. When it was time to eat, you thought you were in heaven. And the most amazing thing about her cooking was that for over thirty years, there was always consistency in both taste and delight. You can only get that kind of guarantee from something when passion, time, and care are invested in it.

WISDOM KEY

ENCOURAGEMENT COMES FROM THE MOST UNLIKELY SOURCE

Those days are long gone, but just writing about them makes me absolutely grateful for her taking the time to take full advantage her Now Moment as an incredible mom and wife for so many years. I believe that these same principles can apply to your personal moments in life. No one wants a life that's thrown together with no time or energy spent cultivating experiences. We look for people who have this richness in their lives, and we too want to be people full of depth, vibrancy, and creativity.

I truly believe that if you embrace your Now Season, live on purpose in your Now Moment, and put knowledge, insight, and wisdom into action that the taste and aroma of your life will fill your home and community with a richness beyond compare.

In Summary

There is no reason to wait to live in the Now. Staying on the sidelines will not allow you to gain more in your life and to fulfill your purpose. You need to take a close look at why you are not doing it now. For some, it is laziness. For others, it is apathy. Additionally, people often wait for the victories and do not recognize the positive things they have already done. This is especially true of honoring the small things that occur every day—that can make a huge difference in your life.

Practice

1. *Answer these final questions to gain insight that will help you Do It Now.*

   • *What are the little things in life that have helped you on your path to Now?*

   _____

   _____

   _____

   _____

   _____

- *What is holding you back from doing what you need to do and want to do?*

_____

_____

_____

_____

_____

_____

- *Are you lazy or late? If so, how can you stop?*

_____

_____

_____

_____

_____

_____

- *What will it take to get you off the sidelines?*

_____

_____

_____

_____

_____

_____

- *What can you claim victory about that will help you move on?*

_____

_____

_____

_____

_____

_____

CONCLUSION

Thank you for taking this journey with me as a teacher and a student. I know that many of the ideas I have talked about in presenting The Now Way of Life may seem new to you. Yet I also know that they will seem familiar. You have within you the knowledge, insights, and wisdom to meet the challenges of life and find more.

You have the ability to live within your Now Season and Now Moment. You have the ability to live on purpose. You have the ability to help others and gain the help you need. You have the ability to build a community of support. You have the ability to truly appreciate the everyday small things in life.

We all know that life does not give anyone a championship ring. However, if you take a good look at your life and what you've pulled through, you will see that you have earned one.

When you fought through raising that kid by yourself, you earned a championship ring. When you pressed your way through that terrible sickness that was trying to take you out, you earned a championship ring. When you fought through a dysfunctional home, molestation and abuse, you earned a championship ring. When you put yourself through school working two jobs, you earned a championship ring. When you created a family and treated your spouse with love and respect, you earned a championship ring. When you made a decent career for yourself that gave you satisfaction and provided for your family, you earned a championship ring.

These are the accomplishments you need to acknowledge and embrace because they give you the energy and encouragement that you need to continue to go in your Now Season. This is not a time to throw in the towel or back up. It's a time to press forward, and to press forward stronger. There are greater things that are getting ready to happen in your life, and you need to be there to accept and receive them because there are more championship rings to gain.

You lack absolutely nothing. All you need to do is wake up and have faith. When you do, life will still have its challenges. There is no doubt. But you will see them through a new lens. You will see them as ways to help you grow and discover opportunities beyond your imagination.

Most importantly, you will learn to count it all joy. With that, I lovingly share the lyrics from my song "Count It All Joy."

Count It All Joy

I can't see the air still I can breathe
It's here but it's invisible
Just like when I'm blessed my heart doesn't see
Til after the miracle but I'm learning to trust
Your merciful love

Count it all joy whatever comes I will surrender
Father let your will be done
You know all I need you've called me by name
So I'll walk through the dark hurricane
Ride through the fire long as I can hear your voice
I will count it all joy

I'm learning the night is only the start of the most beautiful day
And when my world is torn apart
I know I can look to your grace
But I'm learning to trust Jesus
You are more, more than enough

How can I unbreak a heart and point them to you
If I couldn't say that I've felt that way
And it's something that I've been through

These and other products are available on our website:
www.JAVENONLINE.com
and on iTunes and wherever digital music is sold

Follow @JavenOnline